The Ancient Maya and Their City of Tulum

The Ancient Maya and Their City of Tulum
Uncovering the Mysteries of an Ancient Civilization and Their City of Grandeur

Copyright © 2011 by Bonnie Bley.

All rights reserved. No part of this book may be used or reproduced by any means, graphic, electronic, or mechanical, including photocopying, recording, taping or by any information storage retrieval system without the written permission of the publisher except in the case of brief quotations embodied in critical articles and reviews.

iUniverse books may be ordered through booksellers or by contacting:

iUniverse
1663 Liberty Drive
Bloomington, IN 47403
www.iuniverse.com
1-800-Authors (1-800-288-4677)

Because of the dynamic nature of the Internet, any web addresses or links contained in this book may have changed since publication and may no longer be valid. The views expressed in this work are solely those of the author and do not necessarily reflect the views of the publisher, and the publisher hereby disclaims any responsibility for them.

Any people depicted in stock imagery provided by Thinkstock are models, and such images are being used for illustrative purposes only. Certain stock imagery © Thinkstock.

ISBN: 978-1-4620-6272-0 (sc)
ISBN: 978-1-4620-6320-8 (ebk)

Printed in the United States of America

iUniverse rev. date: 12/22/2011

The Ancient Maya and Their City of Tulum

Uncovering the Mysteries of an Ancient Civilization and
Their City of Grandeur

BONNIE BLEY

iUniverse, Inc.
Bloomington

To Ken, Kevin, and Samm ~ Thank you for your love, support, and encouragement.

To Jo, Lisa, and Nickie ~ Thanks for a great girls trip. Without you, this book would never have come to light.

To Sue, Leslie, John, and Tamara ~ Thank you for being my writing support group and inspiring me.

To my Maya Indiana Jones, aka Carl de Borhegyi ~ Thank you for sharing your excitement and expertise of the Maya with me.

To Elliot Abrams and David Webster~ Thank you for your useful insight for portions of this book.

"We live in an age whose spirit is to discard phantasms and arrive at truth, and the interest lost in one particular is supplied in another scarcely inferior; for the nearer we can bring the builders of these cities to our own times, the greater is our chance of knowing all"
~ John Stevens

TABLE OF CONTENTS

List of Illustrations and Tables

Preface

The Maya are indeed a mystifying and unique ancient civilization and with the approaching date of December 21, 2012, they are at the forefront of daily conversations.

In 2009, I took a trip to Mexico and had the chance to visit the ruins of Tulum. This archaeological site is one of great beauty that takes your breath away. After a two hour guided tour of the site, I yearned to know more about this mystical civilization. Searching for answers led me frustrated with more questions.

I knew there had to be more people out there like me: people searching for understandable answers to the ancient Maya and this great city. This led me to research my curiosities for more than a year. During my quest for the truth, I had the privilege of speaking with Maya experts Carl de Borhegyi, Elliot Abrams, and David Webster. They graciously shared their vast knowledge and expertise with me and lend insight to this book about many aspects of the ancient Maya.

Having all my answers fulfilled, I wanted to share this information with others who are intrigued by the ancient Maya. This book is an original and informative work based on my personal experience and research on the ancient Maya civilization and culture. It was written to satisfy the curiosities of the occidental tourist yearning for answers about these complex indigenous people.

Bonnie Bley

"What we don't know about the Classic Maya is a lot. This is why they fascinate us, and why they are so useful to us. Since we began to rediscover them in the mid-19[h] century the Maya have been shape-shifters—peaceful or warlike, ruled by benevolent priests or by ambitious kings, skilled tropical ecologists or great despoilers of landscapes. We can imagine them as strange and exotic, and at the same time like other ancient civilizations, or even like us. Decipherment of the inscriptions and a great deal of sophisticated archeology done over the past 40 years have begun to pin them down, so we can no longer bend them into any forms agreeable to us. Nevertheless, there remain many gaps in our knowledge that make them still seem enigmatic and romantic, and that we can fill up as our imagination dictate."

David Webster

TIME LINE

➢	4236 B.C.	Earliest date recorded in history with the beginning of Egyptian calendar
➢	3114 B.C	Maya Long Count calendar speculated begin date
➢	2600 B.C.	Nomadic Maya tribes make their way to Guatemala via the Bering Straits
➢	2000 B.C.	Maize is domesticated
➢	2000 B.C	Beginning of Olmec "Mother Culture" Civilization
➢	1800 B.C.-300 B.C.	Pre-Classic Maya period
➢	753 B.C.	Roman Calendar founded by Romulus begins
➢	700 B.C.	Maya writing is developed
➢	600 B.C.-501 B.C.	Maya civilizations move into Mexico
➢	300 B.C.	Maya adopt the idea of society ruled by kings and nobles
➢	300 B.C-250 A.D.	Late Pre-Classic Maya period
➢	45 B.C.	Julius Caesar reforms the Egyptian calendar and it becomes the new Julian calendar
➢	100 A.D.-1521 A.D.	Cult of Quetzalcōatl, Venus, and mushrooms
➢	250 A.D-900 A.D.	Classic "flourishing/flowering era" Maya period
➢	300 A.D.	Dated stele is used by the Maya
➢	600 A.D.-800 A.D.	Maya culture and art reaches it's peak
➢	900 A.D.-1500 A.D.	Post Classic "collapse and abandonment era" Maya period
➢	968 A.D.	Beginning of the Toltec Civilization
➢	1195 A.D-1442 A.D.	Period between first serious outbreaks of civil wars
➢	1224 A.D.	Itzá "idol worshipers" Maya arrive into Mexico in the Xel-Ha, Mexico area
➢	1325 A.D.	Beginning of the Aztec Civilization
➢	1517 A.D.	The first Spanish arrive in the Maya area
➢	1519 A.D.	Hernán Cortés reaches Mexico
➢	1521 A.D-1821 A.D.	Spanish invasion and colonial period of the Maya areas
➢	1542 A.D.	Spanish establish a capital city at Mérida in Yucatán
➢	1582 A.D.	Pope Gregory XIII reforms the Julian calendar and begins the Gregorian calendar
➢	1697 A.D.	Last remains of Maya civilization destroyed by Spanish in Yucatán
➢	1821 A.D.	Mexico gains independence from Spain
➢	1839 A.D.	John Lloyd Stephens discovers and examines Maya ruins in Central America
➢	1847 A.D.	Yucatán Maya rise up against Mexico in the War of Castes
➢	1910 A.D.	Mexican Revolution
➢	1950 A.D.	Stephan de Borhegyi begins radiocarbon dating
➢	1952 A.D.	Yuri Knorozov begins decipherment of Maya codices

Introduction to Maya

The ancient Maya originated somewhere around 2600 B.C. among nomadic tribes in North Central Petén region in Guatemala, when Asiatic people made their way into North America using the Bering Straits when Alaska and Siberia were connected with a land bridge. From there, they migrated into the regions of Western Honduras, Guatemala, the entire Yucatan Peninsula, and vast areas of Chiapas from North America where they settled and lived in small family bands. After settling in these areas they started cultivating maize and began to abandon the nomadic way of life to settle in villages surrounded by cornfields.

During the Pre-Classic period (1800 B.C-300 B.C) their population began to grow and they started to structure and organize themselves. They banded together in large groups from which high ranking chiefs and kings emerged.

Their society became fully organized at the beginning of the Late Pre-Classic period beginning around 300 B.C., and the rise of kingdoms began to function throughout the ancient Maya lands, with four main levels: the nobility, the priesthood, the common people, and the slaves. They were separated by territory and region and for the next thousand years the principles of kingship dominated Maya life.

The Maya civilization was made up of separate regions with a common culture. They had no centralized political leadership so each of these regions or "kingdoms" was under the control of a *halach unic* or "true man". His functions were primarily political and militarily as he was responsible for controlling the regional boundaries. They established a common culture by developing and incorporating elements borrowed from their neighbors.

The communities near the capital were considered "in the realm" and were brought into the fold of the kingdoms, which included outer lying areas ranging from sizable towns, small villages, and extended family farming compounds. They were brought into one kingdom or another and each region became a highly organized society. Kingdoms held populations between 25,000 and 50,000 people which included the outer lying citizens who were as far as a two to three day walk to the king's palace.

The Classic Period or "Golden Age" of the ancient Maya is considered to have begun around 250 A.D. and lasted until 900 A.D. This period is sometimes referred to as the high point or flowering age for the ancient Maya as a civilization. Art, science, construction, and cosmology reached new levels of excellence. Civilizations wide use of the dated stele (a prepared surface on the face of a building, a rock, etc., bearing an inscription or the like) started sometime around 300 A.D.

Highly organized at this time the Maya were spread across an almost continuous territory consisting of three general areas: The tropical rain forests of the lowlands (including northwestern Honduras, the Petén region of Guatemala, and into Belize), the mountains of Chiapas, and the entire Yucatán Peninsula which was the heart of the Classic Maya civilization.

Around 325 A.D. the Maya culture began to develop and spread while external influences disappeared. The typical corbel arch was used in buildings and important dates referring to history and myths were recorded in hieroglyphs. Culture and art reached their peak between 625 A.D. and 800 A.D. in such areas as the calendar, astronomy, architecture, sculpture, and pottery; numerous cities and ceremonial centers were founded.

Nearing the end of the Classic period, their civilization began to experience serious problems. Populations of major cities started dropping excessively as they began to abandon their cities. New construction and maintenance of existing buildings ceased to continue and a collapse of a culture took shape.

The Post-Classic period (900 A.D to 1500 A.D.) is defined by deterioration in the quality of fine art and science. The southern cities were abandoned and many of the ancient Maya moved north toward Tulum, Cobá, and the northern lowland cities. Starting in 976 A.D. the Maya tradition became mixed with the Toltec, originating from central Mexico.

Eventually, all the cities were abandoned and the Maya went back to farming as they had been doing before their civilization was created. They stopped building temples, the population declined, and they became fragmented into competing states that were easy prey for invading forces from the north. The Toltec had become the ruling elite of the Maya in the Post-Classic period and added their gods to the Maya pantheon. The Toltec, however, assimilated with the Maya as they learned to speak Yucatec Maya, and made way for the Aztec civilization which began in 1325 A.D.

The Pre-Hispanic Maya were one of the most amazing civilizations of their time, with clearly defined social order. The elite devoted themselves to trade, war, and religion. Architects, who belonged to the same rank, planned buildings while stonemasons were in a socially inferior class along with governors' servants and the different craftsmen.

While Europe still slumbered in the midst of the Dark Ages the ancient Maya became experts in astronomy with incredibly precise observations; they mastered the study of time and calendared systems. They also created hieroglyphic writing, ceremonial architecture, structural design, mathematics that included the concept of zero, socio-politics, and economics.

It is thought that they inherited the inventions and ideas of earlier civilizations like the Olmec. The Maya adopted and adapted several features of Olmec culture, including architectural elements and the basic number and calendar system that would later become the accurate Maya calendar. While that may be true, the Maya advanced science to a degree that is still astounding modern scientists. They built a vast empire sized trade network, built roads, performed masonry, developed a unique counting system, and the best written language in all of the Americas. These inventors in the jungle also produced rubberized rain clothing, barkless dogs, and stingless honeybees. They created a highly developed culture with systems of writing, calendars, mathematics, astronomy, art, architecture, and religious, political, and military order. They constructed beautiful stone cities and religious temples all on foot without the aid of beasts of burden, metal tools, or even the wheel, as these had not yet been discovered.

Everything that is known about the ancient Maya comes from their four Codices, the Popul Vuh, their mystifying architectural inscriptions, the practices of their modern generations, and the documentations of the biased Spanish settlers. Our perception of their worldview is not yet complete and open for further explanation. Scholars will agree that the philosophy of the Maya answers most of the basic principles of the universe by incorporating arithmetic, astronomy, observations of time, and the plethora of deities and gods they worshipped. The Maya used science, especially astronomy, as tools to bring light to spiritual truth and deciphering the prophecies etched in the dark evening sky.

Much about the Maya culture is lost forever, although the Maya tried to reinstate their former tradition, they only succeeded in bringing back the use of their language, and when the Spanish arrived on the Peninsula they found a people that had lost its luster.

The tropical climate of Mexico did not preserve the tree bark books buried with priests, and the Spanish conquerors and missionaries of the sixteenth century burned or destroyed the remnants of Maya culture that they found. Nevertheless, archaeologists continue to reveal new aspects of this ancient civilization through present day excavations and scientific digs.

City of Tulum, Mexico

The archaeological site of Tulum Ruinas (Tulu'um in Modern Maya; in Spanish orthography, Tulum), of Mexico sits on 39 foot cliffs along the east coast of the Yucatán Peninsula on the Caribbean Sea. It is located 80 miles south of the popular beach resort city of Cancun, Mexico and is less than a one hour drive south of Playa Del Carmen. It is the site of the Pre-Columbian Maya walled city serving as a major port for Coba and was the last Maya outpost. It is relatively compact compared to many other Maya sites in the vicinity and is one of the best preserved coastal sites.

It is a popular destination for tourists, because of its proximity to modern tourism developments along the Mexican Caribbean coastline, the Riviera Maya, and is easily accessible. Daily tour buses bring a steady stream of visitors to the site. The Ruins of Tulum are the third most visited archaeological site in Mexico, after Teotihuacán and Chichén-Itzá. It is popular due to ease of access and its picturesque view of the Caribbean Sea.

The city of Tulum was built around 1200 A.D. and was at its height during the 13th-15th century, and was one of the later Maya outposts. It had a population of no more than 600 and flourished during the 14th century. It was still inhabited by the descendents of the fallen Maya civilization when the Spanish arrived in the early 16th century. It served as an important trading post for the Post-Classic Maya.

The word "tulum" means "fence, trench, or wall," and is the name given to the site in recent times because of the wall surrounding it, although its ancient name was possibly Zama, a corruption of *zamal* (morning), associated with the dawn. This is an ideal name for the site, as sunrise in Tulum is a superb sight. Juan Diaz, who was on Juan de Grijalva's expedition that reached the coast of the Yucatan Peninsula in 1518, made the first mention of this city. He wrote, "We followed the coast day and night; on the following day . . . we sighted a city or town so large that Seville would not have appeared bigger or better . . . a very tall tower was to be seen there . . ."

The topsoil at Tulum is limestone and no above ground river or water system exists. The Maya got their water supply from underground rivers and sinkholes in the limestone that are natural underground waterways known as cenotes. The sinkholes began as underground caverns dug out of limestone by naturally acidic ground water. When the roof of the cavern collapses, the cenote is then formed. The word "cenote" comes from the Spanish mangling of the Mayan word D'zonot that represents a subterranean cavity that contains permanent water. The Spanish could not correctly pronunciate D'zonote; so the word cenote came to existence. Cenotes can be any shape or size; they can appear as a pond, a tiny shaft, and a crack hole or even a lagoon.

Water that flows into a cenote is called the spring side or upstream area of which the water can flow in and out.

The Tulum ruins are unique for the wall, called the Great Wall, that surrounds the temples, houses, and structures within the inner city of the precinct on three sides. It is this impressive wall that makes Tulum one of the most well known fortified sites of the Maya. This massive wall would have taken an enormous amount of time and energy to build, which shows how important defense was to the Maya when they constructed the site. It protected the city on the landward side by a wall that averaged about ten to sixteen feet in height. The wall is about 26 feet thick and 1300 feet long on the side parallel to the sea. The part of the wall that runs the width of the site was slightly shorter and only about 560 feet on both sides. Combined, the north, south, and west wall on land encloses and area approximately 541 feet by 1263 feet.

The walls of Tulum were once painted blood red, which discouraged possible invaders. For this reason, along with its strategic, defendable location, Tulum thrived, becoming a major trade center while her sister cities fell. Even to this day, the walls and internal structures retain a faint pinkish glow as solemn reminder, whispering of her long lost majesty.

On the Southwest and Northwest corners of the Great Wall there are small structures that have been identified as watchtowers, depicting how well they defended their city. Access into the inner precinct is gained through five very narrow corbel arch gateways with guardhouses on either side of the Northeast gateway and small rooms spaced irregularly along each of the walls. Roads (sacbeob) lead out into the countryside of each of the five gates. Near the northern side of the wall a small cenote provided the city with fresh water. A large number of cenotes are located in the Tulum area such as Maya Blue, Naharon, Temple of Doom, Tortuga, Vacaha, Grand Cenote, Abejas, Nohoche Kinn, and Carwash cenotes and cave systems.

The layout of the inner city of Tulum within the fortress walls is of rectangular shape. It included five houses, four temples, and two watchtowers. The inner city also had avenues and a main street axis. Approximately about 10% of the ruins we know lie within the walls. Not only are they significant of the city, but they are the most impressive.

Many residential platforms of the inner precinct rest on sloping ground and appear to be tilted as the city was positioned in a bowl shaped depression. These platforms were used as foundations for perishable non-stone houses that belonged to people important enough to live with in the walls of the inner precinct, but were not royalty.

The inner city contains the most important buildings and was the big highlight of this city. The main structures are the Castle, (El Castillo), the Temple of Descending god, and the Temple of the Initial Series. The remaining structures consist of temples, shrines, and a platform. The temples are structures 2, 3, 4, 10, and 11. The shrines are numbers, 6, and 7. Number 8 is a platform, most likely used for dances and other spectacles. The temples of the Inner precinct are one roomed buildings except for Structure 4, which has a small shrine. Temples 10 and 3 contain columns inside. The shrines can be distinguished from the temples because they are lower. The platforms, primarily used for dance, have a stairway on two of its sides and were quite common in Maya cities.

2 - Walls of Tulum photo by Bonnie Bley

Tulum's architecture is typical of other Maya sites along the east coast of the Yucatan Peninsula, but lacks the elegance of earlier structures in other cities. Doorways are narrow with columns used as support if the building is big enough. The rooms contain one or two small windows and an alter at the back wall, roofed by either a beam and rubble ceiling or being vaulted. The houses had holes in them to watch the placement of the stars and planets to tell them the seasons of the year, the best times for planting, harvesting, and other important activities. This type of architecture resembles that done at the nearby Chichén-Itzá, just on a much smaller scale.

Tulum has buildings designated for the preparation of bodies for burial. They contain two "XX" figures in the architecture. This symbol was representative of the four cardinal directions, and the diamond formed by the intersecting X's represented the earth. The locations that held the bodies before burial also had the "XX" symbol. Misinterpreting the symbolism of the "XX", the early Spanish explorers mistook them for the symbol of the cross and assumed that the Maya had previous contact with a culture of Christian faith, when indeed they had not.

One very important Maya structure missing from the city of Tulum is the ball court. Ball courts were based at the ceremonial core of the city and the game was played and revered at most of all the other great Maya cities. The absence of the ball court at Tulum could be an indication that there was a shift in the religion.

The Caribbean Ocean lies on the forth side of the walled city making this fortress easy to defend. The heavily secured fortress spurs theories that the people of Tulum were threatened by outside influences, as there is evidence that this was a very turbulent time in Maya history. During this time, power shifted between city-states and there was also a certain amount of warfare. The architecture of Tulum has a significant Toltec influence, but whether this came about through invasion or friendly interchange is impossible to determine.

The Temples of Tulum

Located within the inner precinct of Tulum are one castle, and four temples: El Castillo, The Temple of the Frescoes, The Temple of the Diving God, The Temple of the Wind, and The Temple of the Initial Series.

El Castillo, which means "The Castle", is the largest and highest building among the ruins of Tulum, standing at 25 feet tall. It actually wasn't a castle, but was used primarily for religious and sacrificial rituals. It sits almost at the edge of the cliff on the east side of the inner precinct and overlooks the Caribbean Seas like a frozen sentry. It was built in three different time periods with two platforms, two galleries, and a central access stairway being the oldest part and was later used as a base for the erection of the upper temple. It has three known entrances. A hidden fourth entrance at the bottom of the cliffs far below El Castillo is suspected to exist, but not proven. There are two vaulted rooms, and a pillar supported by two serpent shaped columns.

The first phase of the castle was the central part of the gallery which was filled in and served as a base during the second phase of construction. In the original phase of construction the building consisted of a double gallery over a terrace of walls that sloped in a gradual manner. It was entered by means of a stairway used as its center reinforcement. The narrow inner gallery opened at three points into an outer one which was more spacious.

Another stairway and two oratories were later added to El Castillo which each corridor being at one side of the staircase. The entranceway consisted of three openings divided by a pair of columns in the form of snakes with their rattle tails supporting the top and their heads stretching down to the base. It is understood that the oratories served as a lighthouse or beacon which marks a break in the barrier reef that is opposite the site for the ancient Maya merchant ships navigating along the Yucatan shore. When their torches aligned, it showed the way through the reef. It showed the cove and landing beach break among the sea cliffs that would have been perfect for trading canoes coming in. A grand structure seen from afar, the dominating tower symbolized its greatness of the people that built it.

The third phase of El Castillo is a small addition and contains nothing at all, but consist mostly of walls. The ancient Maya might have used it as a solar calendar, as the portals face in all four cardinal directions.

3 - El Castillo
Photo by Bonnie Bley

Arguably one of the most intriguing buildings at the site is the Temple of the Frescos. This temple is thought to have a great social and religious importance to the ancient Maya of Tulum and is situated at the center point of the inner precinct. Like many of the buildings in Tulum, the temple was built in successive phases. The Temple of Frescos was built in three stages which is said to be representative of the three stages of the Maya universe: heaven, earth, and hell.

The first stage is a rather basic structure and it contains a single chamber with an alter. Niched figurines of the Maya diving god or Venus deity decorate the façade of the temple. The entrance of the Temple of the Frescos is decorated with human figure's head pointed downward.

The second built stage consists of a gallery with an entrance formed by several columns decorated with stucco figures. Part of the gallery was filled in at a later date with stone that was used to strengthen the base to support the upper part of the temple. A stone platform carved with a human figure, contains a sign indicating the year it was added but has not yet been deciphered yet. In each of the corners of the temple's façade there is a stucco mask of an old god with decoration around the eyes, a hooked nose, a prominent chin, and a down turned mouth. They are thought to possibly represent Chaac, the god of rain, or perhaps Itzamna, the creator and giver of life. On a rectangular platform in front of the Temple of the Frescoes is a carving with a human figure and in the top right hand corner the sign of a year that also has not yet been deciphered. Its paintings are Toltec style which was one of the most important finds on the peninsula. The rising sun illuminates its center column during the equinox, and it is positioned to the west for its use as an observatory. On the exterior fertility symbols and beautiful masks are found with vestiges of the original paint.

The last upper part of the temple, displays the typical outward sloping wall architecture. It has simplistic moldings and a single chamber which contains a small alter at one end and a curved neckless bottle shaped dome.

4 - Temple of Frescos
Photo by Bonnie Bley

The original temple contains mural paintings that were protected by the gallery. Murals of black, brown, blue, and green vegetable colors are painted on the interior. Although there has not been an official interpretation of the meaning of the murals in the Temple of Frescos, it contains symbolism to the fertility of nature, birth and rebirth, and even their involvement in a Venus/mushroom cult.

Red painted handprints can be seen to the left of the door of the upper temple. The red handprints that appear on the Temple of the Frescos are a recurrent phenomenon in Maya architecture, known to be in ruins all over Central America. John Lloyd Stephens mentions them several times in "Incidents of Travel", noting "the shiver of connection they convey, the inevitable parallel drawn between the temple's ancient builders and the living human being standing before it as physical proofs of a divine intervention in this city's construction. Were these the handprints of a god, taking physical form to bestow his blessing and approval on the faithful?"

The left hand appears to have seven digits. It is claimed to be a characteristic of the grandfather god, Itzamna—along with the supernatural height that would have been required to place the prints where they are.

There is also a pragmatic theory to the seven digit handprints. Bloodlines were highly valued by the ruling class to allow intermixing with common stock, so people with deformities or handicaps, were considered special and unusual. They were sometimes granted different types of religious and political authority. They valued and even revered certain deformities. Art depicting midgets carried atop people's shoulders like household gods have been observed by scientists. The mummified corpse of the great King Pacal, the architect and ruler of the Chapas city of Palneque, was discovered to have seven fingers, so it can be hypothesized that these might even be his handprints.

5 - Red Handprint on Temple of Frescos photo by Bonnie Bley

There are numerous images and carvings of the diving god in Tulum; however, the Temple of the Diving God is the only building that bears its name. A youthful winged diving god descending from the sky is carved in a niche over the doorway of the western entrance of the temple.

The temple served as place of worship and is located on the northern end of the inner precinct. It stands on a flat roofed building that was filled in to serve as a base. A staircase leads up to the temple that has a single chamber and a bottle shaped vault. A roof crest built in three parts tops the building.

The temple formerly had a mural painting both on the main façade and on the southwest and northwest corners where there were religious scenes that included the gods of rain, corn, and the sun. Some murals inside the Temple of the Diving God have been restored to show various deities making offerings in a setting that symbolizes the transformation of Venus in the night sky, with Venus, the Sun, and the stars combined with interlaced serpents. A mural can still be seen on the eastern wall that resembles the style that originated in highland Mexico called the Mixteca-Puebla style.

Temple of the Diving God
Photos by Bonnie Bley

The Temple of the Wind was regarded as a place of worship. It stands on a circular platform that is dedicated to Ehécatl, the god of the wind; thus the name Temple of the Wind. The round platform is thought to symbolize birth as an aspect of Venus, as the Morning Star, reborn after passing through the Underworld. The temple was built on a natural rise on the cliff, north of the cove at Tulum. The temple has a single room, with the entrance on the north side. It has a vaulted roof where remains of a stone sculpture were found.

Temple of the Wind
Photo by Bonnie Bley

The Temple of the Initial Series lies to the southeast of the inner precinct. It faces north and has an entrance to a single room. Originally, stucco figures stood on either side of the entrance, but were found broken to pieces and was dated as 564 A.D. Inside are the remains of a small alter in which Stele 1 had been in place. The stele found by John Lloyd Stephens is what this temple was originally named after. The building was named after this stele, since this is the date of the Initial Series calculation.

The Houses of Tulum

There are four important structures deemed as "houses" inside the walls of Tulum. The term "house" in regards to the ruins is not the same residential house in the same aspect by today's meaning or standards. Houses in the Maya society were reserved for the elite, their families, and their servants. They were used more for ceremony preparation and rituals rather than actual "living space". Kitchens, living rooms, bedrooms, and bathrooms were not "rooms"; instead those were located in shared societal areas.

The House of Columns or "The Palace" is without a doubt the largest residential building in Tulum. Nobles and spiritual leaders of the ancient Maya society inhabited this three-story structure 279 feet long by 115 feet wide and has numerous small chambers. The original structure of the House of Columns was shaped like an L. A west wing was added later due to the population growth demands. A narrow room with small windows contains a shrine that would have been used for rituals to influence the gods or pay homage to their ancestors. The house is decorated with carvings and images honoring deities including the diving god. The House of Columns would be in comparison to the White House in Washington, D.C., or like a United States Governor's house.

The House of Halach Uinik stands on a large raised platform and has an entrance with four columns and a square pillar which were not part of its original feature. The rooms of this house are larger than in any other building in Tulum. A roofed shrine with a direct entrance to it is located in a rear room and the shrine sits against a dividing center wall. An additional column and pillar were added for roof support at a later date to save its sagging roof. A thatch awning is there to prevent further water and sun damage to stucco figures that lie beneath it. A passage on the left leads to a set of stairs which includes a combination of Toltec and Maya architectural designs and contains one of the most beautiful sculptures in Tulum; a descending god over the main doorway. It is believed that light over the temple's façade produced effects that were a vital part of the temple's architecture and ceremonial use. During explorations of the ruins, remnants of incense burners and fragmented earthenware were discovered in the house which would be indicative of burial ceremonies.

Located opposite the Temple of the Frescos is the House of Chultan, which stands for "dug out collector for rainwater". This structure today hardly looks like a structure as the roof collapsed many years ago. The House of Chultan consists of an entrance with two columns and a wide inner gallery with a small sanctuary in the center. An additional gallery was added with rooms behind and a small doorway. Located in the exact center inside the house there was a stucco figure of a Maya head. A figure of the diving god was also inside the building.

Further into the ruin site past the temples toward the sea, there is a relatively small building called "La Casa del Cenote" or "The House of the Well". As the name implies, the structure was built over a cave containing water (a cenote), however, due to its close proximity to the sea, it is too salty to drink. The building is rectangular with a room on each side and a tomb in the middle. At the back of the building there is a small area where its occupants could celebrate religious ceremonies.

House of Columns
Photo by Bonnie Bley

House of Halach Uinik
Photo by Bonnie Bley

Maya Art

The Maya of the Classic period developed a sophisticated artistic tradition, producing painted ceramics, clay figurines, screen fold fig tree bark books of drawings, and hieroglyphic writing. In fact, Maya art is the most highly refined in technique and design of any Pre-Columbian civilization.

Most of the surviving artifacts and inscriptions of the ancient Maya tell the stories of nobility, celebrations of life and death, birth and rebirth, inheritor assignment, royalties rise to power, warfare, and ball games. Depictions of Maya life and art varied from city to city; however, it is felt that the major differences were caused by outside influences.

The art of the Maya was also used for political purposes. Many of the great pieces of Maya art were commissioned by Maya kings to memorialize themselves and publicize their power as this would ensure their place in history.

The stylistically complex wall paintings found in various buildings, usually painted in blue, red, and yellow figures outlined in black, portray how the ancient Maya deities. Arthur Miller (1974) found many symbols of birth and rebirth in these wall paintings. Motifs through out their artwork include various gods, monkeys, jaguars, umbilical cords, headless bodies, and mushrooms which are symbolic to the aspects of life, death, religion, astronomy, and time.

Art in the ruins of the Maya cities are demonstrated in a mixture of architecture by the design and construction of temples, buildings, and pyramids. Carvings on door jams and stele recorded the history of time. Iconic stucco figurines were sculpted into their elaborate temples and castles. Sculpture as it was used in architecture, reached a superior quality incomparable in the history of the Americas. Art, sculpture, and architecture went hand in hand to the Maya. Art was the area of expertise of the elite that was supported by the ruling class. These artisans were not only were they well educated, but also they dedicated their time entirely to art production.

Ceramic and figurine artists used a mixture of finely ground pigments of pounded stone, minerals, and water. The main colors were brown, white, yellow, black, red, and white depicting images of rituals, myths, geometric designs, and hieroglyphs. Ceramics were used as tableware, currency, and as offerings to the dead.

The ancient Maya also excelled in carvings of jade, wood, bone, and shell and took great pride in their artwork. They carved intricate masks dedicated to the dead, often made of or inlaid with jade. They adorned almost everything with paint and carvings, including pottery and temple steps. Additionally, they accumulated rare art pieces from afar by trading one form for another using their trade network that extended throughout Mesoamerica.

Investigators use the art of the ancient Maya not only as tools to unlock the mysteries of the indigenous people but to pinpoint the movement of groups from one place to another, track cultural patterns, establish dates, and determine the importance of the ruins. This is possible because different regions created different forms and styles of art at different times.

A few of the estimated two hundred mushroom stones that escaped destruction, despite the concerted efforts of misdirected Catholic missionaries. The smaller mushroom stones are the ones found with metates, which were presumably used for grinding the sacraments prior to use (Borhegi 1961).

11 - Mushroom stones

12 - Maya Art

First Contact with the Maya

On his fourth and final voyage to the Americas in 1502, explorer Christopher Columbus sailed along the Yucatán shoreline between Santo Domingo and Honduras. As he voyaged he could see Tulum rising in its crimson hued grandeur high atop the cliffs above the Caribbean Ocean, however, it wasn't until 1511 when the very first Spanish landed in this area.

In 1511 a Spanish ship was sunk by a storm off the Caribbean coast near Tulum. Out of the fifteen survivors, Jerónimo de Aguilar and Gonzala Guerro were the only two men who eluded being worked to death as slaves, becoming sacrifices, or falling to disease.

Jerónimo de Aguilar lived for seven years as a slave to a Maya lord drawing water, working in the fields, and carrying heavy loads on trading expeditions. During this time he learned to speak the language. Learning the Maya language was useful to him as he became chief interpreter when he joined forces with Spanish conquistador Hernán Cortes.

Gonzalo Guerro led a much more exciting and different life than that of Aguilar. He started out as a slave to the Maya but earned his freedom after proving himself in battle. By tattooing his face and piercing his ears he took on the same appearance as his newly accepted people. He had gained the respect of the Maya and took his place among them by marrying a Maya princess and having three children with her. These were the first documented mixed race children of the Maya. Later he became the chief mayor of the Maya town Chetumal. When Cortes came to the Yucatán, Guerro refused to join his forces and fought against him.

In 1517 Francisco Hernández de Córdoba took three ships and 110 men on an expedition for new land and slaves for Cuba. He found buildings and a civilization far ornate and superior to anything he'd ever witnessed. However, he was met with hostility and was driven off by Maya troops under the command of none other than Gonzalo Guerrero.

An expedition lead by Juan de Grijalva in 1518 in search of gold and new slaves to take to his Spanish settlements in Cuba sailed past Tulum. The sight of this walled city amazed the captain and crew, with its buildings painted red, blue, and white and with a fire on top of the main temple. Grijalva experienced unfriendly reception and he failed to collect fortunes of gold. He returned to Cuba a disgraced man and Hernán Cortes was then commissioned in 1519.

Further successive Spanish expeditions took place after the arrival of Hernán Cortes until the Spanish had successfully taken control over Central America and Mexico. Some 75 years after the conquest, Tulum was abandoned, but was still visited over the years by

13 - First Contact photo

Maya pilgrims. It was used from time to time as a place of shelter and refuge for Native Indians during the War of Castes.

During the 17th and 18th centuries, the Caribbean coast was considered a savage place with not much to offer for potential settlers. Many stories of violence and hidden treasures of legendary pirates, like Jean Lafitte and Henry Morgan aka "Barbadosed" roamed the seas of the Caribbean.

Because of its location, Western scientists of the late 19th century became aware of Tulum, and excavations started in the early 20th century. The Tulum archaeological site was put on the map when Maya world pioneers, J.L. Stephens and Frederick Catherwood visited the long lost site in 1841. At that time the temples were crumbling and covered in jungle vines and bramble. Tulum became known to the world when they published their book "Incidents of Travel in the Yucatan". Frederick Catherwood's brilliant detailed illustrations of El Castillo became world famous.

The Carnegie Institution of Washington organized expeditions in 1916, 1918, and 1922 led by Slyvanis Morley and other noted researchers. In 1937, members of the Mexican Scientific Expedition studied various sites on the east coast of the Yucatan peninsula, including Tulum. In 1938 Miguel Angel Fernandez began the work of investigating and restoring the ruins. Excavations of Tulum also took place in 1951 and 1955. Finally through present day, the National Institute of Anthropology and History, through the Southeast Regional Center, is continuing investigation and maintenance of this important Maya archaeological site.

Maya Trade

"The most important economic institution of the ancient Maya was the centralized market"

Brainerd, Morley, and Sharer 1983:249

Both coastal and land routes were centralized at Tulum which is apparent by the number of artifacts found in and near the site that show contact with areas all over Central Mexico and Central America. Between El Castillo and the Temple of the Wind at Tulum, there is a break in the cliff that forms an easily accessible cove with a beach of fine sand. By reasonable assumption, Tulum's ideal ocean side is the area where most fishing boats and trading watercrafts arrived and departed. Facing the cove there is a walkway and several low platforms that some experts have defined as their possible market area.

Tulum was the gateway for the sea borne trade of the time. People living on the coast provided shells, salt, dried fish, and pearls for the Chiapas highlands, Guatemala, and El Salvador, or else for Central Mexico and other peoples living in what today are Panama, Costa Rica, and Columbia.

The ancient Maya created an extensive network of trade routes linking different points in the region, which they used for transporting local products such as honey, tobacco, vanilla, rubber, feather, and jaguar skins. Merchants, who belonged to nobility, controlled trade and they transported goods using slaves over land routes and large canoes up to 53 feet long for river and sea trade. Products were usually traded for the produce of other areas, although they were also bought using cocoa beans as currency.

The Yucatan was the greatest producer of salt. The coast is abundant in coastal salt flats. The dry season (January to May) allows for inland saline filled swamps to recede, leaving residual salt encrusted mud. It is estimated that 24,250 tons could be produced annually. The demand for salt and the abundance of the resource in the Yucatan brought forward rigid attention to the salt trade.

It is often believed that the salt industry did not fully develop until a significant population increase during the Classic period. Experts resolved that the Maya primarily relied on the salt industry for economic and aggriculture support through trade because many of the the Maya cities existed in agriculturally poor conditions.

Salt was frequently used for ritual and medicinal purposes. It is suggested that salt was used as a "cold" medicine for curing fevers, and is also believed to have commonly been used during childbirth and death. A midwife would offer salt to the mother for birth pains. A salt water solution was sprinkled throughout the house following the death of a family member.

A controversial issue among experts is whether salt was used as a currency in ancient times. The fact that many other parts of the world were using salt as a form of currency supports this concept. However, Spanish reports during the conquest suggest that it was more an item of small scale barter, rather than a major monetary unit.

The word "jade" evokes exotic images of highly decorated Chinese Emperors for most people, but few realize the rich jade history of the Americas. To the Pre-Columbian people of Mesoamerica, specifically the Maya, jade meant life, fertility, and power. The association of the aristocracy with the brighter greens indicated that they valued jade above all other materials, including gold and diamonds. Just as bright green jade was reserved for Chinese emperors, in Mesoamerica bright green jade was reserved for kings and royalty. The ancient Maya made the following objects of jade: beads, pendants, breastplate ornaments, ear flares, buttons, spangles, mosaic masks, and plaques.

As an example of its desirability, Aztec leader Moctezuma gave the Spanish conquistador Hernán Cortés four jade beads as tribute, with the counsel that each bead was worth two loads of gold. The Spanish conquistadors, lusting only for gold, dismissed these treasures as nothing more than green rocks.

Obsidian (a shiny black piece of volcanic glass formed when lava cools above ground) appear to be some of the more precious stone found near Tulum, although it was not a natural stone for that area, it would have traveled to the area from Ixtepeque in northern Guatemala, which was nearly 430 miles away. This huge distance coupled with the density of obsidian found at the site shows that Tulum was a major trading center of the trading for the stone.

Housewives used obsidian to gather and prepare food, farmers used it to harvest crops and butcher animals, warriors and hunters used it to tip spears and lances, nobles used it for bloodletting ceremonies and wore it as ornaments and priests used it in their bloody sacrificial rites. The elite had it polished and used it for mirrors, vases and figurines. It is sharper than the finest surgical instrument, and can be reworked over and over to maintain its sharp cutting edge.

Textiles were among some of the goods brought to Tulum by sea that would then be dispersed inland. Typical exported goods included feathers and copper objects that came from inland sources. These goods could be transported by sea to river systems that could be taken inland giving seafaring canoes access to both the highlands and the lowlands. Copper artifacts from the Mexican highlands have been found near the site, as have flint artifacts, ceramics, incense burners, and gold objects from all over the Yucatan.

The Yucatán was one of the richest areas in Mexico by the 1880s with Merida being the commercial central. After the introduction of the synthetic rope the economy began a spiral decline in the 1920s. Salt production, small scale fishing, along with harvesting products like mahogany, red cedar, and natural gum remained as the source of sustaining economic growth until the development of tourism.

Tourism was initiated in Mexico in the 1970s and as of the year 2000, became the worlds leading destination for travelers with earnings above eight billion U.S. dollars.

Maya Appearance

hat did ancient Maya men and women hope to see when they looked in their obsidian mirrors? Through their artwork and the study of their physical remains, we can begin to understand what motivated their search for physical perfection.

Beauty was a way to display social, if not moral, value among the Maya. They went to extreme lengths to transform their bodies. The wealth they invested and pain they endured to create what they considered to be beautiful bodies to reflect their social beliefs make our modern day obsession with beauty less excessive. Like us, the Maya indulged in self deception about appearance, preferring to let artistic depictions conform to their ideals rather than reality. The Maya saw what the Maya wanted to see when they looked into their obsidian mirrors: green and blue jewels, perhaps a few daubs of red paint, and the youthful vigor of agricultural fertility.

Maya kings, noblemen, and aristocrats, bored holes in their front teeth and inserted decorative pieces of stone, especially green jade and glossy black obsidian. All Maya filed points on their teeth to make their mouths look more appealing.

Chronologically, the practice of dental decoration arose in the Pre-Classic period and remained a widespread custom until the beginning of the Post-Classic period. Dental decoration was slightly more common amongst females. Present data suggests that the dental mutilations were imposed on frontal teeth of persons more than fifteen years of age. Incrustation, which was dominant among men, occurred at an age slightly above fifteen. Filing continued throughout their adult life and was generally preferred among the female population. There was not a technique or pattern exclusive of either sex.

The Maya and other ancient peoples in the Native Americas practiced head flattening as a mark of social status. Head flattening is the practice of shaping the skull by binding an infant's head. Typically the skull would be bound and wrapped tightly between two boards to form an elongated conical shape. After two days the flattening was enough to be permanent. Head flattening did not interfere with brain function as the brain in infancy is malleable and would conform to the new shape of the skull. Head flattening was done for several days after birth to the children of priests and nobles in order to ensure this mark of beauty.

Another mark of beauty that was promoted was crossed eyes. This was achieved by hanging a ball or strand of beads from their children's bangs in the center of their forehead. It is amazing that the Maya took great strides in creating an appearance which is considered by today's standard as birth deformities.

It is suspected the men wanted to look like "Pakal the Great", who ruled the city of Palenque. The earliest carving images found in his royal palace emphasizes his flattened head. His depicted body reveals a slim physique. He had luxurious hair, which he wore in thick, layered braids trimmed to blunt ends in the front and tied in the back. It flopped forward like corn silk surrounded by leaves at the top of a healthy maize plant. His tomb within Palenque's Temple of the Inscriptions provides a clear view of the standard of beauty to which ancient Maya men aspired.

Long hair was stylish for the Maya for both sexes. Men donned their own mullet of sorts by cutting the sides short and wearing the back long. Their bangs were burnt off too accentuate their elongated heads crafted in infancy. Women had lush heads of long hair that was most always pulled up into one or more tight ponytails or braid to showcase their pointed heads as well. For special occasions the elite Maya would decorate their ponytails and braids with brightly colored ornaments and ribbons. In addition to their carefully styled hair, wealthy Maya men added elaborate feathered headdresses, that were crafted to look like the head of a jaguar, snake, or bird and were covered with animal skin, teeth, and carved jade. Servants and slaves had their hair cut short as a visible mark of their inferior status.

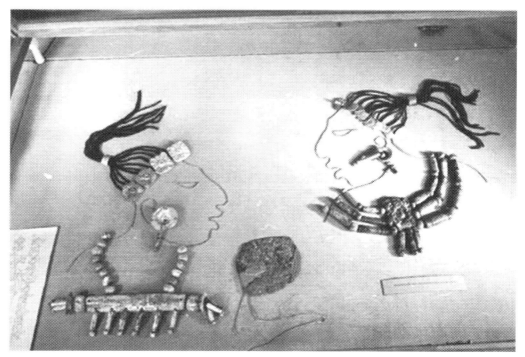

14 - Maya Appearance Photo

Both men and women pierced their ears and tattooed parts of their bodies. Tattoo designs were painted on the body, and then cut into. The paint and scar formed the tattoo. The process was said to be extremely painful, and for this reason tattoos were a signs of personal bravery as the process caused infection and temporary illness. After marriage, some of the Maya applied tattoos to their face and body.

For special occasions and ceremonies less permanent decorations of body paint marked their status. Black and red body paint was a profoundly honored color for warriors while humans to be sacrificed were painted blue.

The jewelry worn by the Maya was rich in variety and astonishingly beautiful. They made jewelry from many materials without metalworking skills. Men wore nose ornaments, earplugs, and lip plugs made of bone, wood, shells, and stones, including jade, topaz, and obsidian. Necklaces, bracelets, anklets, and headgear were made with jaguar and crocodile teeth, jaguar claws, and feathers. Women and children wore less elaborate necklaces and earrings of similar materials.

Men and women basically wore the same kind of jewelry, except women did not wear the lip or nose plugs. Nose plugs symbolized special status among elite men during the Classic Period. Beyond facial ornaments, men typically wore more jewelry than women. They wore many strands of beaded collars as well as single strand bead necklaces with pendants, heavy ritual belts, and ornate earplugs. Earplugs were two piece earrings in which a ring would be secured in the ear by a thick plug usually of semiprecious stone. The earplugs were so heavy they distorted the ear lobe.

Their beauty was also enhanced by wearing fashionable clothing. The fabric used for clothing held great importance among the Maya. The type of cloth and the decoration applied to garments indicated the wearer's status in society. Those of high status wore gauzy cotton dresses over contrasting slips, elaborately decorated dresses cinched at the waist, and sleeveless patterned undergarments with blouses while the poorest members of society wore very plain clothes.

The dress of women was more variable than that of men or children. They wore skirts with or without a scarf tied to cover their breasts. Men wore loincloths, breastplates, and tunics. The climate was so warm that most often a loincloth was the only garment men would wear. Children on the other hand were for the most part naked.

Loincloths were made out of strips of fabric wound around the waist and between the legs, leaving flaps hanging in the front and back. They were made out of an eight-to ten-foot length of cotton cloth and called an "ex". The poorest men would wear a plain ex, but wealthier men would wear an ex made from patterned cloth and adorned with embroidery, feathers, or fringe. Men of wealth and power could wear cotton, while poorer men could only wear loincloths made of maguey fiber, a fleshy, spiny, leaved plant fiber. Those wearing the wrong type of loincloth would be severely punished.

During colder weather, cloaks (called pati) were worn by both the men and the women. They were made from various materials and tied around the shoulders. The highest ranking Maya men draped elegant pati of jaguar skin or feathers from a quetzal bird around their shoulders. Their extravagantly decorated cloaks swept the ground. The poorest people wore plain cloaks woven from the fiber of maguey which reached no further than their knees.

Tunics were sometimes were also worn by the men of Maya. Made of a woven rectangle of cotton, wool, or plant fiber fabric with a hole in the center for the head, tunics resembled loose, sleeveless pullover shirts that hung from the shoulders to within a few inches above or below the knee. Tunics were either left open at the sides or sewn leaving holes near the top fold for the arms to slip through. Tunics could hang freely or be wrapped at the waist with a sash. Like loincloths and cloaks, a tunic signaled a person's social status by the quality of its fabric and richness of its decoration.

The Maya were barefoot most of the time; however, foot coverings did make the rugged terrain easier to manage. Maya royalty and soldiers wore various styles of sandals. Typically these sandals were made of leather from a goat, llama, or sheep, or plant fibers and tied to the foot with leather or woven fabric straps. As with other garments worn by the Maya, the decoration of footwear indicated social status. The wealthiest members of society could wear sandals dyed with bright colors dabbled with beads of gold or silver.

Eventually alteration to the traditional clothing styles occurred with the infiltration of foreigners into the Maya culture. The clothing history of the ancient Maya has been pieced together from oral histories and archaeological excavations, or scientific digs to uncover past cultures.

Medical Practices of the Maya

Holistic by nature, Maya medicine is classified as a medic-religious healing tradition. It was a blend a science and religion. It takes into account not only the physical ills of the body, but also the effects of the spiritual attitudes toward life, living, emotions, depression, anger, fright, ect., and recognizes that they are intertwined. It was their primary understanding that medicine had a connection with calendars, astronomy, and astrology.

The ancient people understood that the mind was very important, and they were focused in their approach to medicine on the relation of the mind and the body. By definition, a reference to the mind indicated an affiliation to the spirit. Body and spirit were not separated in any medical considerations.

The Maya interpreted health as "balance" whereas illness and disease were considered an "imbalance". A central medical related idea held that "balance" was affected favorably or adversely by diet. It was highly influence by the seasons, and varied by age, gender, personality, and exposure to environmental temperature levels.

The concept of "life force" or ch'ulel was profoundly essential to the medicine of the Maya and was the first of the six principles of Maya medicine. This life force was everywhere. It permeated from mountains, rivers, houses, plants, to people, and was said to come from a spiritual divine authority. Ch'ulel binds everyone and everything together. It is a main goal for the Maya healer to balance the flow of ch'ulel in the body. Maya healers also maintained that praying would direct ch'ulel to where it was needed.

The second principle was that separation between the body and the soul, between the physical and spiritual realms, was absent. Ch'ulel represented that everything was linked and unified. The physical and spiritual worlds were at opposite ends of a continuum surrounded by medicine which aided the spirits in the healing processes.

Recognition of natural cycles and the veneration of plants was the third principal. Maya healers talked with plants, as many herbalists do in other traditions. Certain plants choose the healer and they develop a very special relationship. These particular plants that aid the healer in treating the sick, particularly in difficult cases.

The fourth principle recognizes that healing is an integrative and comprehensive approach with everybody, including the healer, the patient, spirits, and plants working together to deliver healing. No single element was more important than the other, with the exception of prayer.

The status of the blood was the fifth element. It helps determine if the origin of the illnesses was physical, spiritual, or emotional and decides the course of treatment.

The sixth principle was the concept of hot and cold as it applied equally to illnesses, foods, and plants. Fevers, diarrhea, and vomiting are examples of "hot" diseases while cramps, constipation, and paralysis are examples of "cold" ones. Examples of hot foods are garlic, onions, pepper, and ginger while cold foods include cheese.

The general idea of hot and cold was most important when they had to chose which plants to use in treatment as "hot" plants treated "cold" illnesses and vice versa. Maya healers maintained that many illnesses were a result of quick temperature changes, such as drinking "cold" drinks with "hot" foods causing shock to the system which led to gastrointestinal problems.

There are several names for what might have been called "specialties" in medicine and it was used it in many different ways. Each name worked directly with a specific body part, and referred sometimes to the mind as well. They sutured wounds with human hair, reduced fractures, and used casts. They were also skilled dentists and surgeons. They filled teeth with iron pyrite and made prosthetics from jade and turquoise.

The Maya bonesetters believed that they had a natural ability, and that their hands "acted of their own accord in locating problem areas." Their approach was pragmatic and non-supernatural. Osteologists of ancient times relied on their hands to guide them in diagnosing and treating injuries using a combination of experience and intuition. They would listen to the patient's narrative, look for deformity, reddening, edema, bruising, and range of motion to determine the type and location of the injury. In order for their hands to glide smoothly over the area, they pressed and watched for signs of deep bruises, sprains, dislocations, or fractures. In many cases massage and limb movement was the main treatment, however, fractures required the use of traction, pressure, and immobilization to reset the bone.

The medicinal use of cocoa, both as a primary remedy and as a means to channel herbal medicines have been documented since the Pre-Classic period. Three logical purposes can be identified: 1) to help gaunt patients with weight gain; 2) to stimulate nervous systems of spiritless, exhausted, or weak patients; and 3) to improve digestion and bowel movements as cocoa fought the effects of stagnant or weak stomachs, stimulated kidneys, and improved intestinal function. Anemia, poor appetite, mental exhaustion, lack of breast milk production, tuberculosis, fever, gout, kidney stones, impotence, and decreased libido were also treated with cocoa.

A cocoa derived paste was used for neutralizing the taste of bitter pharmacological additives. In addition to cacao beans, preparations of cocoa bark, cocoa butter, leaves, and flowers have been used to treat burns, bowel disturbances, skin irritations, abrasions, and cuts.

Maya Religion

Maya religion is extremely complex; however, it did not begin that way. In its simplistic form it answers the questions of the innocent child asking "Where did we come from and what happens to us after we die?" It is closely related to Catholicism with similar beliefs of a creator god, the trinity, and resurrection of the dead.

To the Maya science and religion were one and the same and every aspect about it was dualistic in nature. Their impressive system of mathematics and astronomy was intimately related to religious rituals. The harmony between science and religion is evident in the duties and functions of the ancient Mayan shaman, the Ah Kinob. At the heart of Maya philosophy was astronomy and mathematics and they were considered to be "priestly" inventions. Theologians of the Maya civilization also served as its scribes, mathematicians, astronomers, and intellectuals.

The interaction between the living and the gods was the responsibility of the shaman and royalty. The shaman controlled learning and ritual, and were in charge of planning all facets of Maya life. This was done in order to keep harmony and aid the gods in their work of ruling the worlds. They were responsible for calculating time, festivals, ceremonies, fateful days and seasons, divination, events, cures for diseases, writing, and genealogies. Maya rituals were scheduled far in advance using astronomical and astrological science. The position of the stars and planets depicted how life would be conducted. Sexual abstinence and fasting were observed before and during major events and rituals.

Maya religion infiltrated all aspects of daily life. The rituals priests prescribed, the celebrated holidays, the idols, their ordinary diet, and the cadence of life were all religious in origin. Every material object in the Maya world, as well as every moment in time, had divine worth and godly significance. Additionally, the interplay between the gods and humankind were reasonably manifested in daily routines.

The Maya Viewpoint of Life and Death

The ancient Maya believed that life and death are cyclical, like the seasons and astronomical cycles. They believed that the physical world was unavoidably tied to the supernatural world by the gods who live in that world. The cycles spiral through time without beginning or end and when one ended another would begin. All of this was left to the desire of the gods. In order to understand the Cosmos of the Maya there needs to be a belief in the "other" world, the unseen world of the gods as they lived in the physical world but also recognized that life was connected to the "other" world.

The Maya worshipped their ancestors, and in doing so, they worshipped the gods. From early times on, the dead were painted red and buried underneath their houses, in which the family continued to live. Masks were used at ceremonies and at burial to protect the deceased from the dangers of the underworld.

The Maya believed that everything had a soul, which explains why many of their material belongings were found broken to pieces, as this was believed to release its soul. They were buried with goods of all descriptions that could be of use to them in the afterlife, especially to help make their way through the different levels of the underworld. The more goods they were buried with, the better off they would be.

The way in which a person lived their life did not determine their life in the afterworld. It was the manner of the way they died that determined their destiny in the afterlife. Nobles and their servants were the exception to this rule as nobles became one with the gods in death and dwelt in the night sky with the gods. Warriors who died or were killed during battle and women who died during childbirth earned the right to join the sun god in the sky.

Suicide was the most revered way of death to the Maya. Giving their life to the gods was the most precious gift they had to offer. Many rulers and people committed suicide on their 52nd birthday if they were still alive.

Death from natural causes or disease was not desirable to the ancient Maya, because the dead did not automatically go to paradise. When a person died from a normal death, their soul would have to pass through the nine levels of the underworld before reaching the realm of the death god.

Maya Concept of Creation

There are a few creation stories that the Maya believed, although similar in theory starting with creator gods, but the most popular and accepted Maya concept of a creation story is that of the creator gods Tepeu the Maker and Gucamatz the Feathered Serpent.

The story is that the two creator gods are surrounded by the still waters of the sea. The gods engage in a dialogue and begin the act of creation. Through their speech and thoughts earth and mountains are raised out of the water. Animals were then placed upon the earth, but they lacked the voices and understanding that was needed to worship and nourish the gods. Tepeu and Gucamatz decide that man must be created.

Their first attempt at making man was to create them from the mud of the earth. However, the mud men were too soft and weak. They did not speak or hear, and also did not know how to worship their creator gods. Soon the mud people were destroyed.

In their second attempt to create man, the gods consulted two diviners who suggested creating man out of wood and women from rushes. This new breed of people could speak and multiply, but they lacked the understanding of their world and makers, so Tepeu and Gucamatz sent violent rains and a great flood to destroy them. Fierce demons, animals, and their own household utensils joined in the attack. It is believed that the survivors who escaped this demise became monkeys.

After the destruction of the wood and rush people, the creator gods created humans from maize brought in by four animals from the mountains. The maize was ground into nine drinks from which the first four men were made. Although these new humans of maize worshiped and nourished the gods, they were too knowledgeable and wise, like the gods who created them. For this reason Tepeu and Gucamatz clouded their eyes, limiting the vision of the present human race and weakened their great understanding of the world.

The newly created men settled down to live on the new land grateful to their creators and sang them songs of worship and praises. The four men were rewarded with wives to be their mates.

Maya Concept of Heaven

Heaven is a celestial realm of peace and rest.
"A place of delights, offering an abundance of food and drink and freedom from pain and suffering"

(Sharer 1994:525)

The heavens consisted of thirteen levels with one god assigned to each level and each level housed a multitude of deities. The heavens were supported by five trees known as sky bearers with four in each cardinal direction and one in the center. Earth from which these trees grew is the first layer of heaven. Earth was perceived to be a large wheel surrounded by divine water, which is the ocean that extends to the horizon. The moon and clouds make up the second layer of heaven. Stars that lie stationary in the sky constitute the third layer. The deity Citlallicue ("She of the Starry Skirts") resides in this third level of the heavens. Occupying the forth level is the mighty sun. Venus, the "Great Star," inhabits the fifth level. The sixth level is called Ilhuicatl Mamalhuazocan, or "Heaven of the Fire Drill," which is thought to represent Orion's Belt. This layer is also where comets ("Stars that Smoke") come from, and where the fire serpents bring forth the sun each day from the east. The seventh level of heaven is the green or black heaven, filled with violent winds and storms. The eighth layer is blue heaven, which is where dust is located. The ninth layer is known as Itztapal Nanatzcayan, or "Where Stone Slabs Crash Together" and is home to the thunder. Layers ten, eleven, and twelve respectively represent the colors white, yellow, and red. The thirteenth and final layer is called Omeyocan, and is where the dual male-female god, who created space and time, resides.

The thirteen levels of the heavens had successive journeys influenced by thirteen spirits. Creative and nurturing female spirits ruled the odd numbered heavens. Warlike men were the spirits that ruled the even numbered heavens. Each level of heaven represented the way in which a person died. For example; people who were murdered resided at a different level as those who had drowned. People whose death journey started out in hell (the Underworld) had to outsmart the gods of their realm to be allowed to go to heaven.

The journeys through the heavens can be considered to be both intellectual growth and development of the consciousness and cognizance of the almighty. The thirteen evolutionary leaps through Great Cycle alternate between seven euphoric and progressive light cycles, and six dark cycles. It is suggested that these are metaphorically represented by the seven days and six nights of the creation week described in Genesis, as the Great Cycle describes a creation that is still unfinished. Likewise, symbolically the seven candles of the Jewish menorah are separated by six dark spaces.

The Maya Perception of Earth

In the eyes of the ancient Maya the land upon which they lived was a square that was completely surrounded by water. This earthly plane was situated between the upper world of the heavens and the underworlds of the night and death, which is most often shown in Maya art as a two headed caiman or a turtle lying in a great lake. Earth was also believed to be located on the top of the shell of a turtle, or on the back of a crocodile. Their universe had five directions, or "cardinal directions" relating to the sun's daily course that was delicately woven with the passage of time.

The Maya believed earth was one of three coexisting worlds and earth was the human or concrete part of that universe. Uniting these three planes was the world tree located in the center and it served as a portal between the human world and the other two worlds through which the gods could freely travel. The center of the earth was associated to the color green, as the ceiba tree which represented the great world tree raised in the center of the cosmos. This tree was the transitional place of the supernatural world and the human world. The world tree's skyward branches separated into thirteen levels where most of the benevolent gods in the Maya pantheon, called oxlahuntiku, inhabited the upperworld. Four giant ceiba trees located at each corner of the world hold above the upperworld are suspended over the plane of the earth during the daytime while the four bacabs Mulac, Cuac, Kan, and Bacab, supported the plane of the earth from below.

When the world was created, a pillar of the sky was set up; the white tree of abundance in the north, the black tree of abundance in the west, the yellow tree of abundance in the south, and then the great green ceiba tree of abundance was set up in the center, as green was the characteristic color of the earth's center. The trees helped establish their encompassing living environment. The trees provide the material from which they built homes and tools. It was the source of many foods, medicines, and essential commodities such as chocolate and paper. They provided the fuel for cooking fires and the soil enriching ash that came from the cutting and burning of the forest. Trees were the source of shade in the courtyards and public places of villages and cities, and provided homes to the animals of the forest. It is logical that the Maya chose this central metaphor for human power.

According to the Maya model, the earth spins around a central axis consisting of a huge ceiba tree, or "World Tree", whose trunk extends into the heavens toward the North Star and whose roots delve deep below the plane of the earth. The heavens themselves rotate around this axis as a giant celestial sphere, making the Maya model of the Earth highly reminiscent of a spinning gyroscope.

At night these celestial planes rotate around the earth's axis, giving humans a view of the Underworld and temporarily concealing the Upperworld. Some scholars give into the idea that the celestial sphere is fixed in place, and that the sun travels through the abyss of the Underworld at night and returns at dawn and each day in as a cycle of destruction and rebirth.

The sun god, springs forth from the mouth of the earth in the morning, scales through the thirteen levels of heaven, arriving at the uppermost level at noon, then descends to enter the Underworld at dusk thus, uniting the three worlds of the Maya.

Journey Through the Maya Underworld

The Mesoamerican underworld, also known as Xibalba "place of fright", is situated below the plane of the earth. It is a grim place of darkness and decay and was believed to be the destination of those who escaped a violent death. It was a place of the dead, rather than a hell like place for the punishment of wrongdoing and its ghostly inhabitants were tricksters' more than evil spirits. However, the guilty and the evil hearted were an exception to this rule and were damned to suffer an eternity in the underworld.

Death was thought to be a journey with the possibility of rebirth or a chance to be resurrected or deified into the heavens. Burial sites were situated accordingly to provide access to the underworld and some of them even went so far as to bury the dead in caves. Living relatives of the deceased prepared the dead for their journey through the underworld by burying them with valuable earthly possessions. Jade and stone beads were given to the dead to serve as currency. Maize was placed in their mouth as a symbol of rebirth and also to feed them during their journey in the underworld. They were also buried with animal shaped whistles, made from rocks, to help the dead find their way through the underworld. Dogs were considered guides for the dead spirit, so if they had a dog it would be sacrificed and buried with the deceased. In some instances, young attendants to royalty would be sacrificed to accompany their lord on his journey through the underworld.

The Maya believed that when people died, they entered the underworld through a cave or a cenote with the conceived notion that the Milky Way was the road to Xibalba. Xibalba's realm was vast and its path was very steep, thorny, and forbidding. It was filled with obstacles and included many distinct hazards that the dead had to defeat, such as treacherous waters, harsh mountains, obsidian blades, and blood and heart sacrifices. These hazards had to be withstood before reaching the lowest level known as Mictlan. Once they reached Mictlan, they offered up their belongings to the god of the ninth realm and his wife.

There were six houses seated in the underworld and their purpose was to kill or humiliate the people placed in them: Dark House, was completely dark inside; Bat House, filled with dangerous screeching bats; Razor House, filled with sharp blades and razors that moved on their own; Jaguar House, was filled with ferocious hungry jaguars; Fire House, was filled with extreme heat and blazing fires; Cold House, was inundated with loud rattling hail and bone chilling cold. The deceased had the opportunity to earn their way out of the underworld by being able to pass the tests of the houses. They could also overcome or trick the underworld gods and their trials and tribulations through mental ability, strength, and tenacity, such as beating them at their own ball court games.

Dark House

Bolt House

Razor House

Jaguar House

Fire House

Cold House

15 - Xibalba

Gods One Death and Seven Death were most important in the underworld. Owls symbolized death and these two gods had owls that served as their messengers. The owls depicted in Maya art work appear to be great horned owls, with the names of Shooting Owl, One-Legged Owl, Macaw Owl, and Skull Owl. The owls would observe the human realm and notify the death gods of the next victim by screeching.

One Death and Seven Death also had ghastly and malicious death lords that were assigned specific duties. Scab Stripper and Blood Gatherer drew blood from people. Demon of Pus and Demon of Jaundice made people swell up, become jaundiced, and made pus come out of their legs. Bone Scepter and Skull Scepter made people die from emaciation and edema until they withered away to nothing but bones. Bone Scepter and Skull Scepter were the staff bearers of Xibalba and the staffs they carried were made of bones. Wing and Packstrap took care of "sudden death". They would strike people on the neck and chest causing suffering until blood was vomited. Demon of Filth and Demon of Woe (also sometimes referred to as Bloody Teeth and Bloody Claws) gave people sudden fright whenever they had filth, trash, or grime in the doorway of their house. Once the person was knocked down from sudden fright, these two demons punctured the person until they crawled to the ground and died.

The nine lords of the night also resided in the underworld. The specific names of these lords has not yet been determined or deciphered and are only referred to as G1-G9. The most important of these lords was G1 and G9. G1 is thought to be a monkey god representative of the trinity and rebirth, while G9 is thought to be the god Kukulcan/Queztalcoatl representing the decapitation or execution of time. These nine lords each ruled over a specific night in a cyclical pattern, with every nine nights repeating itself. These gods could traverse freely through the three worlds of the Maya and they had a direct effect on the world of which they presided.

Not only did the deceased and the gods move through and make journeys through the underworld, but Venus, the sun, and the moon also made passages through the underworld. The entire sky replicated its movements to the inhabitants of Xibalba and they needed the help of the Maya to be reborn each day.

Sacrificial Practices of the Maya

The deliberate taking of human life was viewed as necessary to render certain ritual occasions holy, such as the ascension to the throne by a new ruler or the dedication of a new building. Since the gods had offered up their own blood to create humankind, sacrifice was thought as an ultimate means to repay the gods.

Human sacrifice was originally reserved for kings and royalty. Prisoners of high ranking status that were captured in war between Maya cities were scheduled for ritual sacrifice. The seizing of an adversarial ruler was an extremely treasured sacrifice and this life contributed additional value to the event. Captured enemies of lower position were not worthy of sacrifice and were used as slaves instead. However, later on sacrifice was perpetrated on prisoners, slaves, women, and children. Orphans and illegitimate children could be purchased for sacrifice. Criminals of society, however, could not be offered as sacrifice. Execution was reserved for them, and execution was not to be confused with sacrifice.

The practice of human sacrifice most likely did not originate with the Maya and it is more closely tied to the warlike influence of the Toltec. Before the Toltec era animal sacrifice was common practice. Turkeys, dogs, squirrels, quail, and iguana were considered suitable offerings to the Maya gods. Animal sacrifices were made using a knife or sharp obsidian stone to kill them, then they would inspect their intestines to see whether the gods were happy or not.

Blood letting and self mutilation were performed by the elite class of the Maya during most important ceremonies such as, the end of a bundle of time, anointing religious articles, the dedication of monuments, or birth of a royal heir. The Maya were obsessed with blood and it was a huge part of ceremonies and rituals. Bloodletting was performed by cutting or piercing a part of the body such as the earlobes, tongue, or penis with ceremonial tools such as obsidian blades and even with stingray spines. Every major political or religious events involved bloodletting because it provided a medium by which the gods could be called upon to witness and actually participate in the ceremony.

The blood was drawn in a manner that it would spill into a bowl filled with wadded up pieces of bark paper. The blood stained paper was then burned. The smoke created from the blood of kings and their families sent their human energy skyward. If the gods accepted the offering, then the king would receive divine power in return. Bloodletting was also carried out to appease the gods in times of trouble or to communicate with ancestors and was used as a means of direct communication. Depictions of bloodletting can be seen in the Madrid Codices, lintels at Yaxchilan and Bonampak, and stele from El Naranjo are also described in some documents.

Once the actual bloodletting was over, a pillar of smoke from the burned, blood soaked ceremonial paper was released, and it became a medium for a Vision Serpent to appear. The manifestation of a Vision Serpent has been associated with bloodletting that many have attempted to explain. The Vision Serpent was a hallucinogenic being where ancestors of the victim came out its mouth to speak directly to the Maya. The most logical conclusion is that massive blood loss causes the brain to release an abundance of natural endorphins, which are chemically related to opiates. As the body goes into shock, a hallucinatory vision occurs.

The Vision Serpent can be a logical explanation of the stages of unconsciousness, which was evident during sacrifice. The Vision Serpent more than likely would have appeared between the second and third stage, with death being the fourth stage. In this altered state the victim would have loss of reflexes and movement. The pain of sacrifice would have subsided and the person would have lost the sense of their surroundings. Wavering between what was real and not, a sacrificial victim would easily have slipped into a hallucinogenic state of mind which would be normal with mass amounts of blood loss as the brain is deprived of its richly oxygenated blood supply.

It has also been concluded that sacrificial victims were fed hallucinogenic mushrooms by priests prior to being sacrificed. These mushrooms contained psilocybin which sends the user into a psychedelic transcended state of mind. The effects of the mushroom were much like LSD, and would ease the anxiety of the soon to be sacrificial victim which would explain why these intended victims did not fight back and rebel against being sacrificed. While in this altered state of mind, the Vision Serpent would appear and they could hear the voices of their ancestors.

Sacrifice was carried out in many different ways. In public ceremony decapitation was the usual method reserved for the sacrifice of elite captives, as these people were the most prized. Decapitation was accordant with the connection of the maize god who had been decapitated by the gods of the underworld before being reborn as the first Maya king. It is thought that decapitation of the rival rulers was a climax of a ball game or other events that drew large crowds.

Penetrating the chest cavity and removing the live beating heart was the favored form of sacrifice. The victims were placed face up over a convex alter like stone. The arms and legs of the victim were held by specially designated priests, while their chest was penetrated with a flint knife just below the left breast. The still beating heart was then removed from the chest cavity and handed to another priest, who would then smear the blood on an idol to which the sacrifice had been made. If the sacrifice had been made on top of a temple, the corpse would be thrown down to the courtyard below where priests of lower rank would skin it with the exception of the hands and feet. The skin was then worn by the officiating priest who would dance among the spectators in a dignified and somber manner. If the victim had been an especially brave warrior, his body was sometimes butchered and eaten by nobles and other spectators.

16 - Maya Sacrifice

Bow and arrows were also used in human sacrifice. According to a sixteenth century account "the foul priest in vestments went up and wounded the victims in parts of shame, whether it was a man or a woman, and drew blood and came down and anointed the face of the idol with it". Dancers all armed with bows and arrows "began one after another to shoot at his heart . . . in this manner they made his whole chest . . . like a hedgehog of arrows".

No matter the choice of sacrifice, victims were stripped and their entire body was painted blue before being led into the temple for sacrifice. Blue was used as the sacrificial color and was associated with the rain deities. During times of drought, sacrifices would be made to call forth the rain gods.

The blue color was a vivid turquoise colored pigment known as Maya blue. This specific color has been of interest to both archeology and chemistry scholars. The blue was a very long lasting pigment. It was more durable than most natural dyes and colors. The pigment withstood age, acid, weathering, biodegradation, and modern chemical solvents. Researchers have identified two ingredients; indigo plant leaf extract and palygorskite which is an unusual white clay mineral. It is thought that the leaf extract from the indigo plant and the palygorskite were bound together by copal, which was the sacred incense burned at rituals. This binding agent of the copal is suspected to have kept the color existent for such long periods of time.

Edible offerings were also shared with the gods. Baskets of meat filled tortillas were arranged in front of the god pots with small bits placed in the mouths of the embellished figurines. A porridge of sweetened corn and honey was fed to the god pots and also eaten by the men attending the ceremony. An effervescent chocolate liquid made from cocoa beans was drunk as a final offering.

According to discredited legend, young virgins were thrown into a cenote to appease the most honored gods. According to accepted legend, (supported by the research of archaeologists), gold and jade objects were thrown in to pacify the gods, as were chickens, turkeys, and dogs, with an occasional sacrifice of captives of high rank. Bishop De Landa reported in the sixteenth century "into this well (Sacred Cenote at Chichén Itzá) they have the custom of throwing men alive as a sacrifice to the gods in times of drought, and they believed they did not die though they never saw them again".

All ritual, ceremony, bloodletting, sacrifice (both human and animal) was used to establish a means of communication with the spirit world. Kings and even priests were believed to have supernatural powers and these rituals were used as a means of demonstrating the ruling classes' power and closeness to the gods.

As barbaric and diabolical as sacrifice by the Maya was, they were amateurs when it came to human sacrifice on a massive scale. The Aztecs of Central Mexico had the art of mass human sacrifice mastered. They once sacrificed twenty thousand people in a single ceremony to commemorate the dedication to a new temple and later ate them.

Maya Gods

A multitude of deities exercised authority and strongly influenced the Maya universe. Not only did the Maya honor gods for cities and kingdoms, but they revered gods for every aspect of life. They had gods for days, months, years, and epochs; gods for emotions; gods for professions, gods for animate and inanimate objects; and gods of noble families. Natural elements, stars, planets, numbers, crops, days of the calendar, and periods of time all had their own gods. So many gods existed for seasons of the year, days of the week, and other calendared events that the Maya faith has been called a "solar and temporal cult". Most of the Maya gods were dualistic in nature keeping with the Maya faith. The gods' characters, malevolence, benevolence, and associations changed according to the days in the Maya calendar or the positions of the sun, moon, Venus, and the stars. At least 166 major gods received homage from the Maya priests and figure prominently in texts such as the Codices and the Maya holy book of the Popol Vuh.

To the indigenous people of Mesoamerica, the gods have historically fulfilled a cultural role with their power, wisdom, sanction, and protection. These powers were invoked for all earthly and spiritual transactions from healing, divination, success in agriculture, trade, politics, war, childbirth, grief, and so forth. The gods communicated with the Maya through channeling and visionary dreams. A dream prompted by the gods could be distinguished from a normal dream by the consistent presence of one notable person who says nothing, but stands in the background of the dream that is unfolding. Upon awakening the dreamer realizes that the notable mute person was actually a god influencing and controlling the entire experience revealing a message of importance.

Shaman would often escape to the confines of a dark cave in order to have such godly visions. He would live in the cave without food or sleep and not come out until the gods had spoken directly to him. Once the gods had relayed their message to the shaman, he would exit the cave and carry out the gods orders, whether it be sacrifice someone, build a new temple, or declare war.

The ancient Maya worshiped more than 300 gods. A little over two-hundred of those gods have names, with some having a few different names. The gods were first known as the alphabet gods because in the early days of archeological exploration, when the glyphs and codices were still a complete mystery, no one had a clue what the gods names were, so for administrative purposes, they were identified by the letters of the alphabet. Paul Schellhas first compiled the godly A to Z naming of the ancient Maya gods in 1904, with various revisions appearing over the years. As more information was shed, godologists were gradually able to work out the names of the each god or goddess.

Of all the gods worshipped in Mesoamerican religions, the most significant one with the greatest influence over the people was Quetzalcōatl. He had a variety of aspects and was prominent from 300 A.D. through the collapse of the Aztec civilization in 1521.

Quetzalcōatl is unique in that he appears in Maya history not only as a leading celestial creator god, but has been identified as the iconic priest king Topiltzin Cē Ācatl Quetzalcōatl. He also had his own priesthood following, a cult that was present throughout Mesoamerican city states for centuries.

Quetzalcōatl the man was born in the year One Ācatl, which was religiously significant as this was the beginning of a new 52 year cycle of the Mesoamerican calendar. His birth also corresponded to birth of Christ, although Spanish friars compared Quetzalcōatl to the Catholic figure of St. Thomas.

He promised to return in the year One Ce Ācatl to bring revenge upon those responsible for his renouncement of the throne. It was this exile that brought people to believe that he was a god, as only a god could make such a promise for such a specific date to return from the dead. When Hernán Cortes arrived to the Mexico region in the year One Ce Ācatl, the people believed that Quetzalcōatl's prophecy had indeed come true, and Cortes was mistaken for the reincarnate Quetzalcōatl.

Since Quetzalcōatl was so highly worshiped later rulers of cities took his name as this was important in keeping with ancestral blood lines, however not all rulers who beared this name were a direct linage to Topiltzin Cē Ācatl Quetzalcōatl.

Quetzalcōatl's demise was that he committed suicide on his 52nd birthday. Since he had not died in battle, this was how he ensured his entrance into the heavens. Political order, religious authority, and representing a primary source of culture are what he is legendary for.

Quetzalcōatl (Kukulcan in the Post Classic period of the Maya) the god was the link between the mortal and immortal worlds, the humans and the gods. He was the symbolic explanation linking life and death. Dualistically, he represented many aspects: human and god, Venus and the sun, heaven and earth, life and death.

He played a number of creative roles in Maya mythology: generated the universe, ruled over various cosmic areas, created fire, assisted the wind, and transforms into the morning and evening stars of Venus. He was the symbol of effective governing establishments and sanctified authority in numerous capital cities that deeply influenced the history of Mesoamerican religions for almost 1,500 years.

As a creator god, the story of Quetzalcōatl in essence is that he went to the Underworld in search of his father. He outsmarted the gods of Xibalba and collected together the bones of past generations. He then bled on these bones to create a new race of humans. As a creator god, he had as much power necessary to destroy the world. He was the maker, modeler, and molder . . . a trinity deity.

Quetzalcōatl was a marvelous combination of serpent and bird. He was known as "The Plumed Serpent" and was depicted as a winged rattle snake god. Quetz was a brilliant emerald feathered bird in Mesoamerica, and coatl means "serpent or sky". Some relate him closely to the cycles and as an interpreter to the sacred mysteries of Venus. It is thought that his heart resurrects as Venus, the morning star. He can also be construed to be the Vision Serpent seen during sacrifice and the constellation Orion.

Illustrated by Bonnie Bley

17 - Queztalcoatl

Itzamna was an enigmatic god, but he was considered to be the high god to the Maya. He bears the title of "lord" for his predominate role of king in the Post Classic codices. He was the founding god of maize and writing, also presided over medicine and healing, divination, calendars, and cocoa. He created many things that made life better for humanity and refused to have anything to do with wars, violence, or human sacrifices. In aged form, he is God D in the Schellas Alphabet Gods and was a sky deity related to an aged sun about ready to enter the underworld.

Itzamna was the first shaman and diviner who could open the portals to the spirit world. Kings and shamans would plead with him to open the way so sacred nourishment would flow into the world to sustain humanity.

Itzamna means "Lizard House"; the prefix "itz" can mean "dew" or "nectar". It was thought that Maya priests collected dew to use in their religious rituals. Because of Itzamna's ranking as an inventor god, he was invoked during many different festivals throughout the year, especially during the months of Uo and Zip which were strictly devoted to his worship.

Images of him often contain snakes or mussels and he himself is depicted as an old man with a flower headdress. He resembles an ordinary human being except for his extraordinary size, stature, and stamina. He had superhuman strength, stamina, vitality, and resistance to injury. He also had the ability to tap into and manipulate mystical energies and can be compared to the Greek god Zeus.

Chac, is one of the top ancient Maya gods, and is also known as God B, which represents bursting clouds. He is the god of rain, thunder, lightening, agriculture, and fertility. Since rain was part of every day life he was very important to the Maya. He was one of the longest continuously worshipped gods of ancient Mesoamerica, and continues to be worshipped among the Maya people in present day.

He was part human and part shark, had ears like a deer, had the whiskers of a catfish, and wore a seashell earring. His hair was a permanent knot of tangled confusion, which was quite endearing of him. He wielded a lightening bolt weapon. He existed on the perimeter of the cosmos and marks the way between the natural and supernatural worlds. He brought the rain and could create thunderbolts by hurling down his stone ax.

He was very important for harvesting and growing which the ancient Maya were doing quite frequently. Chac sent rain into the world by weeping from his generously large unselfish looking eyes, and he even taught the secrets of farming at no extra sacrificial cost.

Cizin (*pronounced Ki sin*) aka Ah Puch literally means 'stench or stinking one'. He was the patron god of "the day of the dog". He was the god of death, the underworld, disaster, earthquakes, and darkness and the arch nemesis of Itzamna. He loved to uproot the trees planted by Chac. In Mictlan he burned the souls of the dead. He first burned the soul of the deceased on the mouth and anus. When the soul complained, he would douse it with water until the soul complained again. Cizin was profoundly stupid and susceptible to being easily outwitted by smarter gods, so if the soul figured out how to outsmart Cizin then it was free to go wherever it chose.

He was described as having a fleshless nose and lower jaw and sometimes his entire head may be depicted as just a skull. His body can be shown as a spine and ribs with bleached bones and blood red spots. He was often depicted on pottery and illustrated in the codices in the form of a dancing skeleton, holding a smoking cigarette. Bell like jewelry was tied to his hair and he took great pleasure in causing eternal torture and torment to the damned. He also wore a death collar, his most prominent feature of which consisted of disembodied eyes dangling by their nerve cords. He was frequently depicted with the god of war in scenes of human sacrifice in Pre-Conquest codices or manuscripts and was shown uprooting and destroying trees planted by Chac. After the Spanish Conquest, Cizin became merged with the Christian devil.

Cizin / Ah Puch liked to surface at night and sulk around in a really scary mode. He used his evil bird of bad tidings named Muan, as his personal messenger. If he was not collecting souls of the dead, then he was busy stirring up sickness, causing war, or looking for evil people to help him search for the dead. A putrefying corpse with an owl's head was his favorite outfit to wear. The deeds he did when seeking a victim were far worse than one would care to imagine. The only one way to escape his evil attentions was to howl, shriek, moan, and scream sounding entirely and perfectly convincing as Cizin would assume that you are already being taken care of in another torturous manner by some of his lesser demons. The legend remains today, that when an owl screeches, it means someone nearby will die. The next time you hear an owl screech, take a very deep breath, count to ten, and pray that Cizin is not coming to collect your soul.

Cizin ~ Illustration by Ken Bley

Ixchel, which can translate to "Lady Rainbow" was the goddess of pregnant women, procreation, the moon, the earth, and healing. She oversaw weaving, medicine, childbirth, and protected the fertility of women. She invented weaving, and being partly waterfall she, took charge of downpours. She is also known as goddess O, representing obstetrics.

As an ancient fertility goddess and representation of sensual love, Ixchel was responsible for sending rain to cultivate the crops and when doing so, she was referred to as "Lady Rainbow". She helped insure fertility by overturning her sacred womb jar so that the waters would flow.

Though sometimes thought to be a goddess of catastrophe, especially when she would flood the world, many of her myths show her in a more compassionate light, as a goddess who refused to become a victim of oppression. She was a woman who took charge of her life when faced with adversity. Comfortable with all phases of life, she was honored as the weaver of the life cycle.

The small Isla Mujeres ("Island of Women") and Cozumel were devoted to the worship of Ixchel. Pilgrimages to Cozumel were made to consort and pay homage to her. Many nights she spent on her sacred island of Cozumel nursing women during their pregnancies and childbirth. Ixchel, like other moon goddesses, governed women's reproductive systems so it was quite understandable that she would become the protector of women during pregnancy and labor.

Ixchel encourages us to acknowledge the negative forces affecting our lives. She prompts us to assert ourselves fully in the face of physical or emotional violence that would diminish our sense of self. The night riding goddess spent her energies in nursing the women of earth through pregnancy and labor, taking special care of those who visited her sacred island of Cozumel.

Ixchel's heart belonged to Itzamna. Itzamna, however, seemed immune to her charms. For years Ixchel longed for him, as he would glide across the sky. The more she followed him around, the worse the weather on earth would become. The tides would raise creating floods that drowned the fields and caused the crops to die. She was so in love with Itzamna that she did not even notice she was causing havoc. Their relationship was turbulent, on again, off again, but through their torrid love affairs they produced four sons.

Their four sons were the Babcabs named for the four directions. Each one was placed at one of the four corners of the universe, and was responsible for holding up his corner of the sky. Each brother was associated with a color and with a specific segment in the Maya calendar.

Unfortunately Ixchel's love affair with the Sun God drew the fury of her disapproving grandfather. In his anger he struck Ixchel with lightning, which killed her. For the next 183 days she lay lifeless as hundreds of dragonflies surrounded her body and sang to her. Waking suddenly, she returned to the palace of the Sun God.

Xbalanque and his twin brother Hunahpu appear as a creation account story in the Popol Vuh. They defeated the lords of Xibalba in a ball game in an underworld championship, and in doing so were allowed to retrieve the remains of their father and uncle. Collecting the bones of their father was thought to signify their search for maize. They had many exciting adventures and are known strictly for their ball game defeats and monster slaying abilities. They were seen in the heavens, and every day when the bright sun sets, Xbalanque tosses the stars across the dark empty heavens. Throwing the stars across the heavens was a good way to keep his throwing arm in good condition for his ball games in which he was always competing.

Acan, was the god of wine and all things good otherwise known as intoxication. He was a very noisy and mischievous god who loved to make a fool of himself while under the influence. His name means "groan" and by all accounts he does a good deal of groaning, especially the day after heavy drinking and frolicking.

Acat was the god of tattoos and tattooing. The Maya often adorned themselves in body art, which was of very deep mystical significance. They favored designs of the utmost godliness and did not waste time inking themselves with unimportant or frivolous designs. Instead, they believed having a symbol of a god tattooed on their flesh would give them just the slightest touch of godly essence.

Ixtab was the suicide goddess or goddess of the hanged, which makes it clear that the Maya did not regard life or death with the same views we have today. She was depicted with a rope around her neck. Since the Maya believed that "heaven" lay beyond a suicide, it is believed that this practice may have been quite common. Ixtab would receive the souls of the suicide by hanging into the realm of eternal paradise. Death was closely intertwined with life, for they believed one was first dead, before one was born, i.e. had life. Death was a doorway to life, and life was a doorway to death, thus death and death rituals were quite important in this society.

The god Votan, although not much is known about him, is thought to be quite possibly Quetzalcōatl, just in another form, perhaps during his wanderings of half mythical journeys. Like Quetzalcōatl, he had his own following of priests, and declared himself a serpent. He was the guardian of hollow wooden instruments, and was also known as the old black god of warfare and death. No one is too sure when he was first worshipped, which is why no one remembers who he really is. It was so long ago, that it may have begun before the beginning of time. His admirers loved him unquestionably and called him 'the heart of the cities'. He kept the company of the beloved Ixchel when she wasn't busy chasing Itzamna around the skies.

The Maya Writing System

"Without doubt, the Classic Maya left us with one of the most flamboyant archaeological records of durable and intelligible images and symbols found anywhere, carved and painted on everything from bones to buildings. The intellectual mastery that we deduce from all this material, along with specific kinds of information it conveys, are principal reasons why the Maya are so famous and so interesting to us."

David Webster

Quite possibly the most important key to unlocking the ancient Mayan language are the four codices that were somehow salvaged during the Spanish Conquest. The few that did survive are a valuable source of information. The four surviving codices discovered to date have proved to be a valuable source of information and deal exclusively with religious and astronomical matters. Out of the thirty-one Mayan languages, they are mostly written in archaic Yucatecan, reasonably assumed to be a form of a "high" or "prestige" Classic Ch'olti' language. The Dresden Codex (78 pages, probably written at Chichén Itzá around 1200 A.D.), includes tables of Venus and would be considered to be comparable to an astronomic almanac. The Madrid Codex (112 pages), contains calendared and astronomic charts, but also has several pages dedicated to daily life, use of medicinal plants, and art. The Paris Codex (22 pages), rediscovered in the Paris National Library in 1859, contains information on weather, astronomy, calendared cycles, gods, and history. The Grolier Codex (11 pages), authenticated as late as 1983, contains tables and information pertaining to the movements of Venus.

Early Spanish priests who went to the Yucatán and immersed themselves to learn the language, were overshadowed by Bishop Diego de Landa's campaign to exterminate pagan rites. De Landa was responsible for one of the greatest devastating acts on a culture when he ordered the collection and destruction of most of the written Maya works. The four salvaged codices, writings on temples, ceramics, and pottery are all that remain for archeologists and linguistic specialists to study and decipher.

Interpretation, understanding, and knowledge of the Mayan written language surprisingly began with Bishop Diego de Landa, when he started compiling a key to the Mayan syllabary in circa 1566. His interpretations known as the "Landa Alphabet" consisted of twenty-seven Spanish letters and the Mayan glyphs with similar sounds. De Landa's work in his manuscript "Relación de las coas de Yucatán", lay undiscovered in the archives of the Spanish Royal Academy until circa 1832.

In the 1950s, Russian ethnologist Yuri Valentinovich Knorosov studied the ancient writings and proposed that the glyphs and writings were phonetic and not based on an alphabet; however, Knorosov's ideas were not welcomed by early Western Mayanists, with J. Eric S. Thompson as his biggest opponent. Further progress was made on the many Mayan inscriptions when key figures including David Kelley, Ian Graham, Gillette Griffin, and Michael Coe studied the glyphs and proved Knorosov's research to be correct. Dramatic breakthroughs in deciphering the Mayan language occurred in the 1970s when historians, linguistic specialists, and epigraphers Floyd Lounsbury, Peter Matthews, and Linda Schele identified and decoded the first sequence of powerful Maya kings.

Their writing system was somewhat similar to the ancient Egyptian hieroglyphs and modern Japanese writing, although not related in any form. The unit of the Maya writing system is the glyph, which is equivalent to words and sentences of a modern language. Their writing was written in blocks arranged in columns that were two blocks wide. Within each block, the glyphs were arranged from top-to-bottom and left-to-right. Each block corresponded to a noun or verb phrase.

The writings of the Maya are very difficult to interpret as the glyphs can represent both sounds and ideas. The glyphs must be combined with the context to know exactly how it should be read. Because of its intricacy, the difficult task of deciphering the hieroglyphic writing has not been completed. Due to the variations in the glyphs, their writing needs to be decoded and interpreted rather than just read, as Maya concepts can be written in more than one way and have multiple meanings. Numbers, for example, can be written with symbols or with the picture of the god associated with that number or a combination of the two. There are approximately thirty phonetic sounds in the ancient Classic Mayan language and eight hundred glyphs that are cataloged starting with the letter "T" (J. Eric S. Thompson's system).

They wrote using hundreds of individual signs or glyphs that represented words of syllables that could be combined and sometimes the glyphs were written where an element of one glyph would replace part of a second glyph. These combinations then would form a word in the Mayan language, which included numbers, time periods, seasons, animals, names, titles, events, names of gods, objects, places, and food. Syllabic glyphs were used phonetically to clarify the logograms that had more than one meaning. The glyphs were also used to write grammatical components such as spoken variations that did not have a dedicated logogram in order to conform to the rules of accepted grammar spoken by the native Maya.

Phonetic glyphs stood for simple consonant-vowel syllables. Since most Mayan words ended in a consonant, instead of a vowel, there are many sequences of two consonants within the word. When words ending with l, m, n, j, or h, the consonants were often ignored and an extra vowel was written. This ending vowel was an echo of the vowel that preceded the previous syllable in the word.

Emblem glyphs were reserved for royal titles. These glyphs consisted of a larger main sign and two smaller signs. The smaller elements remain relatively consistent between Maya sites, but the main signs differed from each city in order to identify the different controlled territories and ruling dynasties.

The Maya considered writing to be a sacred gift from the gods and most could not read. Reading and writing was limited to a small percentage of nobles and was jealously guarded. It was thought that reading and writing was a form of communication with the gods, and only the elite of the ruling class were allowed to possess such knowledge. Scribes recorded history, religion and mythology using a complicated system of hieroglyphs, while painters and sculptors depicted both mythical and religious subjects as well as the deeds of governors.

Archaeologists have been studying the writing of the Maya for many decades, but it wasn't until 1962, that the Maya hieroglyphs were first catalogued. Since then a great deal of progress has been made in understanding the glyphs found at ruins and excavation sites. The ongoing work of decoding the glyphs hold promise that many of the mysteries surrounding the Maya may one day be solved.

— 313 —

19 - Maya writing

The Mayan Language

Mayan languages are spoken throughout the indigenous Maya in Mexico, Belize, Guatemala, and Honduras by at least six million people. What was once thought to be the universal language with few distinct dialects has now developed into approximately thirty distinguishable dialects. The languages, while related, are so different that they can be considered completely different languages.

The word "Maya" was most likely taken from the Post Classic Yucatán city of Mayapan. The current meaning of the word "Maya" encompasses the ethnic and cultural traits, rather than linguistics. Maya primary identify with a specific ethnic group, but they also acknowledge a mutual Maya kinship.

The Mayan language is one of the best documented and most studied languages in the Americas. The language began with the base language known as Proto-Mayan being spoken in a basic verb-object-subject word order. From this language, it branched off into four different dialects. The four original branches also extended out during the Classic Period and diversified into separate languages and it is the Mayan languages that exist today that emerged from those original language groups. Expansions of the language occurred due to vast separation into newly settled Maya districts and the collapse of the trade networks of the ancient empires. The result in terms of language was the development of new dialects in isolation and this is easily seen in the evolution of the Maya.

Of the original ancient branches of the Mayan language, Yucatecan Maya, simply known as "Maya" to those who speak it, is the largest surviving language and the most common language of the Yucatán Peninsula of Mexico. The other primary Mayan languages have either become extinct or endangered being spoken only be a few groups in small obscure villages.

The ancient world of the Maya was probably more closely linked linguistically than the Maya of today. The vast differences in the Mayan language prevent different Maya groups of today from understanding one another. A single word in one Maya area can have a completely different meaning in another Maya area. Communication as it once was has not existed for almost eight hundred years

Linguistic differences add complications to the effort of translating hieroglyphic writings. In an effort to reconstruct the family tree of the Mayan language a considerable amount of confusion and difference of opinion has emerged as there are varied interpretations.

Maya Mathematics

Mathematics was very important to the Maya and its sophistication allowed the priesthood to conceive of a universe regular in its rhythms. Mathematics was used for figuring complex computations of time and movement of the planets to the simple aspects of daily life such as merchants using cocoa beans to count out the simplest calculations.

The Maya number system simplistically consisted of only three characters: a dot symbolizing unity which was equal to the number one, a bar representing the number five, and a shell shaped glyph signifying zero. These three symbols were used in various combinations so that even the uneducated people could do simple arithmetic.

There are two exceptional features to Maya mathematics; the use of zero and the assignment value by position, which is why this system was advanced for its time. They understood the value of zero long before most other civilizations, which was an incredible advantage to the Maya to use in advanced calculations. Maya mathematics is one of the most sophisticated yet easy to use mathematical system ever developed in the Americas.

Their numbering system was based on twenty, rather than ten. This means that instead of using the ones, tens, hundreds, and thousands values of modern day mathematics, they used one, twenty, four hundred, and eight thousand as their numerical values.

Numbers were written vertically and divided into rows, with the characters in each row of the column having a value twenty times of the characters in the row directly beneath them. Summing the values of the rows yielded the number represented in the glyph.

Numbers larger than twenty followed the same type of sequence as the numbers below them, but a dot was placed above the entire number for each group of twenty. For example, the number 52 would be written as two bars and two dots (constituting the number twelve), with two dots above that to express additional groups of twenty. The number 40 would be indicated as a shell (constituting the number zero) with two dots above for additional counts of twenty. Their set of numbers is easy to use and allowed uneducated people to add and subtract. For example, to add 8 + 7, there would be a bar and three dots on one side (for 8) and a bar with two dots (for 7) on the other side. The two merge to make three bars, representing the quotient of fifteen.

Just like everything else known to the Maya, numbers had metaphoric meanings, with some of the numbers considered to be sacred and others held special meaning. The number one symbolized unity, beginnings, rebirth, and the original energy of creation. The number two signified duality as most gods were dualistic, with some of the gods being twins. Even Venus, the most important object in the sky was both an evening and a morning star. The number three was representative of the Maya trinity. Symbolism of three monkey and three hearthstone are abundant in Maya art. Also, there are also three stars in the belt of the constellation Orion. The number three is also significantly found in some of Maya archeology as some of the buildings were built in three successive stages. The number four represented wholeness and was associated with the sun. Seven was sacred, and was considered a symbol of endings. The number seven is the midpoint between sacred numbers one and thirteen, so the number seven could be seen as a two sided mirror giving people the ability to see both sides. Eight was also a number of completion or wholeness. Adding sacred numbers one (beginning) and seven (ending), completes eight.

Nine was another special number for the Maya as it symbolized the nine levels of the underworld and also nine lords of the underworld, although it carried a positive energy. God nine of the underworld was Quetzalcōatl, so this number was also considered sacred. Is it any coincidence that there were nine planets in our solar system? That is of course until Pluto was demoted of its planetary status.

Thirteen was considered the divine number and was once called 'the basic structural unit in nature'. Thirteen was the most sacred number as it represented the number of original Maya gods and the thirteen levels of heaven. In correlation, twelve spheres can be gathered around a thirteenth central sphere, and this is the most compact configuration in three dimensional space. A lunar year is thirteen months long, and the moon travels thirteen degrees each solar day. Thirteen was thought to be relatively human as well, as there are thirteen major joints in the human body. The thirteen Maya count days describe a thirteen step course of growth to the planting cycle of a seed. With all of these taken into consideration, the number thirteen was the number that connected the human world to the heavens.

Twenty was representative of the number of fingers and toes a human could count on. The number fifty-two was also considered to be sacred, as it was equal to the number of years in a bundle and was the approximate ending life cycle of the Maya.

Maya Astronomy

Maya astronomy, astrology, and mythology intertwine to form one belief system. In astronomy, they accurately calculated a solar year, compiled precise tables for the positions for the moon and Venus, tracked movements of constellations, and tracked and predicted eclipses. The Maya were obsessed with the sky and their observations led to precise calendars, predictions of solar and lunar eclipses, cycles of the planet Venus, and the movements of constellations. In order for the Maya to understand and predict the various cycles and movements of the sky, they made the best uses of their natural world.

The ancient Maya used observatories, shadow casting devices, and observations of the horizon to trace complex motions of the sun, the stars, and the planets for guidance from the heavens. They used bowls of liquid and observed the solar eclipses in the reflections. Using a forked stick and the naked eye Maya astronomers would take observations and calculate the path of Venus and other celestial bodies. They could calculate with precision events such as solar eclipses and the alignment of Venus and other important planets. They were astronomers before Galileo came to fame, and they were the earliest meteorologists

The Maya highly worshiped the sun, the moon, the planet Venus, and the Orion constellation. These were paramount for survival of the Maya. Celestial events were foretold far in advance and became part of the spiritual platform from which rituals and major events were scheduled. Transfers of royal power for example seem to have been timed by the summer solstice at certain centers. Rituals were timed to coincide with different alignments of Jupiter, Saturn, Mars, and the Moon. They compared past events to movements of the planets to predict the future.

The most important observation in the sky was the placement of Venus, as an evening planet, as a morning star, and an evening star. They tracked the number of days it appeared in the sky, the number of evenings it disappeared from the sky, and its position in the sky. They watched for and documented one of the rarest planetary alignments of Venus, where Venus passes between the earth and the sun, which was visible at sunset for the Maya. They used this to create calendars, plant and harvest their crops, declare war, and several other important aspects of daily life. Images of the diving god and other Venus war decoration is seen carved in buildings, and on stele in Maya cities. Raids and captures were timed by the appearances of Venus. Warfare related to the movements of Venus was in fact well established throughout Maya cities of Mesoamerica.

** next Venus Transit is set to happen June 5/6 2012

photo by Bonnie Bley

20 - Moon Photo

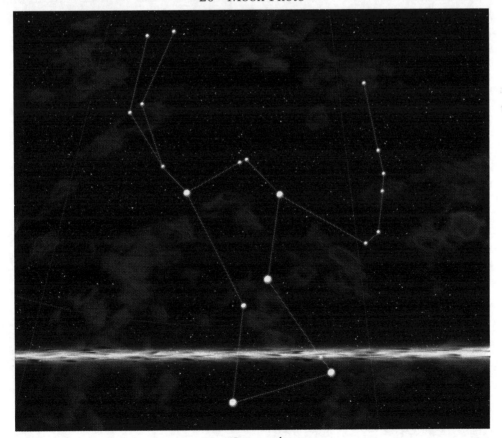

21 - Orion photo

The moon not only affects the tides, but it was used to predict the weather for the Maya. They could predict rainfall by the tilt of the moon and determine the wet and dry seasons. This in turn helped with their agriculture planning. The moon played a very important role in Maya mythology.

Orion was the constellation that was closely observed and fixated on by the Maya. It represented a resurrected ball player in the sky, with the moon being the ball, and Venus representing the head of a decapitated ball player. Orion helped resurrect the sun. The three stars of Orion's belt were considered to be the 'creation' or 'hearth' stones and falls in line with the idea of the trinity. Orion's position just above the equator made it easily visible to the Maya, and in a twenty four time period, Orion sets in the west, passes beneath the earth, and rises again in the east. This constellation gives its viewer the illusion that it is the stars that are moving and not the earth. It dominates the sky in December and throughout the winter.

Other celestial events that could have been tracked by the Maya was Halley's Comet. Seeing this comet shoot across the evening sky, must have been really special to the Maya, especially since it repeats itself approximately every 79.66 years. It is visible to the naked eye and has been recorded since at least 240 B.C. It orbits the sun in the opposite direction of the planets and crosses the path of many celestial objects. The Maya could have mistaken the comet for a planet or a god, but it was indeed predictable and traceable.

Maya astronomers devoted their time to finding harmony in the universe and its recurring cycles of time. They had to make complicated calculations to predict natural events and connect them with the fate of the population.

The Maya Calendar System

he Maya were obsessed with the idea of time and they were rigidly bound to their calendars. It became an obsession around which their daily lives as well as the broader aspects of their civilization had revolved. Their calendars were the center of their cultural life which revolved around the concept of time. They looked to the shifting of the heavens to create their calendars and from these observations, the Maya developed calendars to keep track of celestial movements and the passage of time. Comprehension of Maya history, philosophy, or religion would not be possible without the clues to understand their calendric calculations.

Maya calendars were made possible by the knowledge of astronomical time periods, the possession of a worthy technical system of symbols, and the use of a system of names and numbers. Their calendars were based on a mathematical system using multiples of twenties, which distinguishes them from any other Mesoamerican created calendars. Of all the world's ancient calendar systems, theirs is the most complex, intricate, and accurate. In the science of time, the Maya outdistanced every civilization of the ancient world. The Julian calendar that the Spanish conquistadors brought with them was completely useless to the Maya.

The Maya invented sun time and they discovered a true solar year using natural cues and careful astronomic observations. They thought of the sun as having ages, and we are currently believed to be in the fourth age of the sun. The Maya also had the first lunar calendar. They watched the moon and its movements, and tracked it carefully. They created a cycle of lunar months and lunar years. Their calendars synchronized everything for the Maya. It synchronized time, the solar year, a solar day, lunar months, lunar days, Venus cycles, and other movements of the stars and planets.

The calendars allowed the priests who controlled over society and the nobles to record past eclipses of the moon, and predict when it would occur again. They documented the dates of hurricanes, floods, and other disasters, and believed that these disasters could be repeated on the reoccurrence of specific dates. Since only the priests and a few elite could explain the functions of these calendars it added to their power and control over the lesser lower classes. The Maya life was regulated to a very high degree and there was a special time of the year for everything.

Their obsessions lead them to create seventeen calendars, with four of them being the most important: The Tzolk'in (Sacred Round), the Haab (The Vague Year), Calendar Round, and the Long Count.

Tzolk'in—Sacred Round:

The Tzolk'in is the time period that is called a Sacred Round. The Sacred Round of 260 days moves through time sort of in a repeating spiral that meets the Haab calendar at the end of 52 solar years. It consisted of a smaller wheel of 13 glyphs rotated with a large wheel of 20 days, resulting in the 260-day sacred year. It served as a 260-day almanac. The 260-day cycle is the oldest and most important calendar. As a testimony to the Tzolk'in's symmetry to Maya culture, it is still observed today among traditional Maya groups.

A 260-day cycle is the most fundamental feature of Maya time count. Its invention is pure and simple. The 260-day Tzolk'in is the oldest calendar cycle known in Mesoamerica, dating back to at least 600 BC. While some scholars are still searching for an astronomical basis for this cycle, most agree it was based on the nine-month human gestation period.

It may tie several celestial events together, including the configuration of Mars, appearances of Venus, or eclipse seasons. It is also thought to represent the length of time to cultivate corn. Some insist that it is based on the cycles of Pleiades constellation. However, it's presumed that it corrsponds to no natural time period and is merely the admiration of the numbers thirteen and twenty.

Since the Maya knew that the earth year was a little more than 365 days, they developed the Tzolk'in, which has proven to be extremely accurate. The calculations of Maya priests were so precise that its correction is slightly more exact than the standard calendar the world uses today. The Tzolk'in has thirteen months each containing twenty-six days, making the calendar a 260 day year, which is an astronomical year.

The Tzolk'in is made up of a set of twenty day names and thirteen numerals. The days are numbered one through thirteen, and the names are also given in sequence. A day will not recur until all the numbers and names have run through a complete 260-day cycle. Thus, there is a unique day name for each of the 260 days, and there are no weeks or months. Each of the twenty day names has its own spirit, and its number coefficient speaks to its weakness or strength on that given day

The beginning of the Tzolk'in calendar begins with the first day name, and the number one. The days continue in sequence, with the second day being a combination of a day name and the number two; the day names and numbers combine in sequence until all 13 are used.

Once the calendar reaches the thirteenth day the numbers begin again with one, but the day names move forward with the fourteenth glyph. By rotating like this, the two sets form 260 unique combinations of a day name and a number. Once the end of a cycle of a day name reaches an end, the day names begin anew.

In order to understand how the Tzolk'in works, think of two interlocking gears, with the thirteen numerals spaced around a small circular gear that fits inside of the large gear of day names denoted in hieroglyphics. When the gears lock together at the number one and the day name Imix', then rotate the gears until one and Imix are reached again, this ends with 260 unique days. Those gears spin until the final combination clicks into place, marking the end of the year.

It's easy to see the significance the Maya put in the Tzolk'in calendar. Holy men also scheduled certain events throughout the year based on the Tzolk'in calendar. At the beginning of each period of twenty days, a shaman would count forward to determine when religious and ceremonial events would occur. He would then select the dates that would be the most prosperous or luckiest for the community. Despite its complexity and multitude of functions, the Tzolk'in calendar couldn't measure a solar year, because of this the Maya needed a more accurate calendar to track the length of time that is regarded as a full year.

They had days dedicated to: asking for water, asking for protection for human conditions and illnesses, plan weddings and meeting in-laws, work on community projects, seek wisdom, ask for and give forgiveness, remember the dead, go hunting, tend to the crops, give offerings to the earth, pay debts, and seek counsel.

The Haab:

Haab or The Vague Year, is the solar calendar, which consists of 365 days. It uses eighteen months consisting of twenty days each, with an unlucky five day period at the end of the year which was known as 'Wayeb'. The Haab begins with Maya solar New Year which is thought to have begun sometime in the month of July when the sun peaks. The Haab was in use to around 100 B.C. and it was created to be used in conjunction with the Tzolk'in.

Haab was used for every day events and agriculture, and numbered 365.242129. It's based on the cycle of the sun and was used for agricultural, economic and accounting activities. Much like the Tzolk'in calendar, it's also comprised hieroglyph day names and numbers, however, instead of using 13 month for 260 days, the Haab calendar has 18 months, giving it 360 days.

Maya astronomers noticed that 360 days wasn't enough time for the sun to make it through a full solar cycle. They argued that the calendar should follow the cycle as closely as possible for accuracy, but the Maya mathematicians disagreed. They wanted to keep things simple, in increments of twenty, just like their math system. The astronomers and mathematicians finally agreed on the eighteen months, with five "nameless days or unlucky days". The Wayeb, or Uayeb, is considered one "month" of five days and was considered to be a very dangerous time. The Maya believed the gods rested during that time, leaving the earth unprotected. They performed ceremonies and rituals during this time, hoping that the gods would return once again. Nothing else was done during the Wayeb. Arguments that occurred were believed to end. Those born during this time were believed doomed to eternal misery.

Each month was designated for certain events such as: honor certain gods, prepare for and hold festivals, and renovate temples. The first month of the year was preceeded by fasting and abstinence. The first day of the Haab New Year the Maya celebrated with gift giving and drinking. The last five days of the year were "bad luck" days and nothing of significance was done during those days. Many would go with out bathing or even leave their houses.

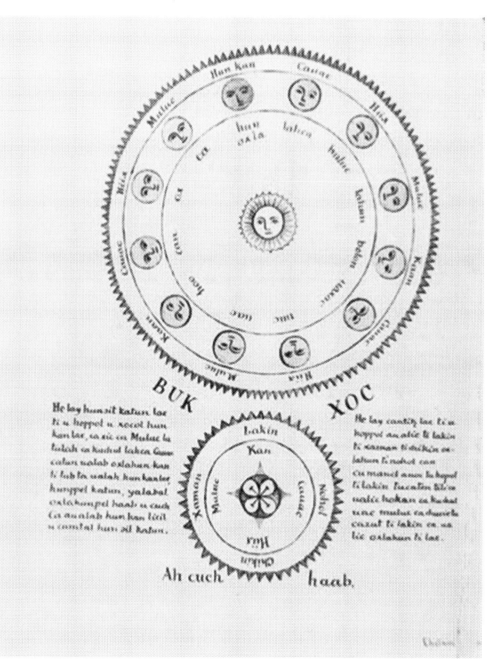

22 - Maya Calendar

The Calendar Round:

One cannot find a Haab date that is not recorded with a Tzolk'in date within ancient hieroglyphic texts. In operation together, the Haab and Tzolk'in create a larger, 52-year cycle called the Calendar Round that was not only used by the Maya but also by every other culture in Mesoamerica.

In the Calendar Round, the 260 days of the Tzolk'in calendar are paired with the 360 days and five nameless days of the Haab calendar. The two calendars are matched the same way the Tzolk'in day names and numbers are. By combining the Tzolk'in and Haab Calendars, the Maya had 18,980 uniquely designated days equivilant to approximately 52 solar years. In order to record history in longer incriments, because the Calendar Round cycle repeats itself once for each lifetime. Fifty two years was longer than the average Maya life span at the time of the Calendar Round's creation.

At the time, the Calendar Round was the longest calendar in Mesoamerica. While this calendar was longer than the Tzolk'in, the Maya wanted to create a calendar that would record even more time. For this reason, the Tzolk'in and Haab cyclical calendars were intercalibrated to create the Calendar Round of 52 years, called the "Binding of the Years". For only once in 52 years or 8,980 days could the combination of the numbers 13, 20, and 365 repeat themselves. The Calendar Round and its cycle were both central and sacred to all Mesoamerican civilizations by combining of all three calendars they could create a time wheel to interpret the past, present, and future. The linking of the Tzolk'in and the Haab occurs every 52 years. This 52-year period of time was called a 'bundle' and meant the same to the Maya as the century means to us.

The Long Count:

The 52-year cycle of the Calendar Round turned out to be inadequate and in order for contemporary historians to record Maya history for generations to come, they turned to the Long Count Calendar the Maya created in order to measure the continual passage of time through the ages. It multiplies up from the other calendar systems and incorporates an era called a "Great Cycle" which lasts approximately 5,128 (Gregorian calendar) years. It is believed to start around 3114 B.C (according to GMT—Goodman Martinez Thompson correlation of dates) and runs to the present age and into the future. The idea that the world may be on its way to an end comes from The Long Count calendar.

Similar to the birth of Christ as a starting point for modern historical dates, the Long Count was not only used to fix dates accurately in time, but also, to correlate the actions of Maya rulers to historic and mythological events and to mark the time of past and future occurrences.

The Long Count, for which the true Maya name is not known, is commonly considered the Maya linear count of days. In truth it is yet another cycle, but its great length of approximately 5,128 years makes it essentially a linear count through all of Maya history.

The Long Count moved backwards in time, recording events. Archeologists have discovered that the date the days that had passed since the time it occurred was based on September 6, 3114

B.C., which pre-dates the Maya civilization. It is uncertain why the Maya would have chosen this day to begin their calculation of time, but it is interesting to ponder and has experts at odds with each other as the actual begin date.

The numeration of the Long Count calendar is divided into five distinct units: kin (one day), uinal (twenty days), tun (360 days), katun (7,200 days), and baktun (144,000 days). The Long Count's version of a year is only 360 days which does not equal a solar year. This means that the Long Count deviates from the Haab by five days every year, making it a completely unique and separate cycle. When the Maya recorded the Long Count days on a glyph it is was written as an introductory glyph, the date, followed by one of the nine lords of the night.

The Maya spoke of eras each equaling thirteen baktuns or approximately 5,128 (Gregorian calendar) years (13 X 144,000 days dived by 365 days of the Gregorian calendar). Each cycle of thirteen baktuns was considered as an "Age" or "Great Cycle", which meant a beginning to a new historical era marked by new emergence and profound change. There are proponents to the theory of an era equaling thirteen baktuns, arguing that a "Great Cycle" or "Era" consisted of twenty baktun (20 X 144,000 days divided by 365 days or approximately 7,890 Gregorian calendar years).

Each era had an attributed meaning correspondent to a particular glyph. A different sun controlled each Great Cycle with a specific destiny for the evolution of those who were present during that era.

It is the Long Count date that archeaolgists correspond to Gregorian dates when determining calendar correlations. It is thought that the basis for the Goodman-Martinez-Thompson (GMT) correlation was based on corresponding dates of the Spanish Inquistion recorded both on the Maya calendar and the Julian calendar. The widely accepted Long Count begin date to date is September 6, 3114 B.C. which is a GMT corresponded date. Determining when the last cycle began, deciphering if each "Era" was thirteen or twenty baktun, and matching that up to a Gregorian date is challenging and controversial to say the least.

The Long Count calendar dates include all five denoted units of time reading from left to right. The first place signifies the number of baktuns since the beginning of the Great Cycle. The second place relates to the number of katuns that have taken place. Then, it continues on to the right with the number of tuns, uinals and kins.

Here are examples of Long Count dates using (GMT correlation date) September 6, 3114 B.C. as the begin date of 0.0.0.0.0 and the lord of the night associated with that day:

Christopher Columbus sets said from Spain for a New World—August 2, 1492: 11.13.12.1.2 G4

Hernán Cortés was greeted by Aztec Emporor Moctezuma II—November 8, 1519: 11.14.19.13.1 G9

American Declaration of Independence was signed—July 4, 1776: 12.8.0.1.13 G6

Mexico became Indepenant from Spain—September 16, 1821: 12.10.5.17.2 G9

World War II began—September 1, 1939: 12.16.5.11.5 G9

American President John F. Kennedy was assasinated—November 22, 1963: 12.17.10.3.13 G1

Assasination attempt on American President Ronald Reagan—March 30, 1981: 12.18.7.14.11 G3

Terrorist attack on America by using commercial airplines—September 11, 2001: 12.19.8.10.1 G3

End of the Maya "Great Cycle" and the fourth age of the sun—December 21, 2012: 13.0.0.0.0 G9

Cults of The Maya

"the Indians (Maya) adored this star more than any other save the sun, and performed more ritual sacrifices for it than for any other creature, celestial or terrestrial . . . . The final reason why their calendar was based on this star, which they greatly revered and honored with sacrifices, was because these misguided people believed that when one of their principal gods, called Quetzalcoatl, died and left this world, he was metamorphosed into that radiant star."

(LaFaye, 1987) In actuality, that star was the planet Venus.

The Maya were extremely superstitious people and people of dedicated rituals. There are three cults that have been associated with the ancient Maya that Carl de Borhegyi and his late father Stephan de Borhegyi have put much time and energy into studying. These cults can be seen as three separate cults, yet one intertwined cult in the same respect. The cults are the Cult of Quetzalcōatl, The Venus Cult, and The Mushroom Cult. Evidence of such cults is seen all throughout Maya art, mythology, and their intricate calendar systems.

The Cult of Quetzalcōatl follows the man, the myth, and the legend. He was the ruler of many aspects of Maya life and Maya worlds. His essence in the world was as a cultural hero and he was the god of many things, including self-sacrifice. Quetzalcōatl's teachings were that mankind must make sacrifices, such as he did, to the deities and transcend from this world in order to achieve immortality. Quetzalcōatl was thought to be deified as the morning star of Venus and with that he brought forth life every day.

Quetzalcōatl's seven stages of priest-kingship was highly revered and honored by the Maya. It starts out with his miraculous birth after his mother had swallowed a precious jade stone, and follows his teenage revenge of his father's murder. They praise his training for the priesthood and his years as a warrior. They honor his ascension to the throne, the fall of his capital, and finally his promise to return one day.

To say that the Maya revered Venus more than any other heavenly body is an understatement. Venus was watched, worshipped, and prayed to. It was worshipped more than the sun or anything else. All aspects of Maya life and religion tie directly to Venus. Buildings were constructed and sacrifices were made in honor of the planet Venus. Symbolism of Venus is seen throughout their artwork and in façades of their temples. Venus represented life, death, and rebirth.

The Maya thought Venus was a resurrected sun from previous world, which is why it was so highly venerated. As the morning star it was thought to bring the sun forward with it everyday.

As the evening star it was thought guide the sun through the underworld, therefore, Venus was responsible for both the life and death of the sun.

The Maya had a calendar entirely devoted to Venus and its movements. It was the most intensely observed planet and its cycle of 584 days was carefully charted and inscribed alongside other calendared reckonings. Venus appears as the Morning Star for 236 days, then disappears for 90 days, then becomes the Evening Star for 250 days, and ends its cycle in Inferior Conjuncture for eight days. Every so often Venus passes in front of the sun and this is known as The Venus Transit, which the Maya also kept track of. Five cycles of Venus is exactly equal to eight solar years, and the Maya were well aware of this configuration.

Mushroom cults were not specific to the ancient Maya, but they have been identified in ancient civilizations of Siberia, Tanzania, Africa, and Easter Island. Deep devotion was shown to the mushrooms as part of an ancient religion practiced in Mesoamerica prior to the arrival of Christopher Columbus. The presence of hallucinogenic mushrooms is apparent in Maya art seen on murals in temples and stone sculptures dated back as early as 300 B.C. Mushroom stones had a ceremonial association with the Nine Lords of the Night and the gods of the underworld.

Mushroom spores are thought to have been dropped to earth from the debris of passing comets. Mushroom rites were likely connected with human sacrifice and ritual decapitations. They were fed to sacrificial victims prior to their deadly demise. These psychotropic mushrooms are credited to inducing transcendent states of mind and altered states of consciousness producing transformable mystical and spiritual experiences that offered long lasting benefits. Eating them led to intense spiritual experiences (an advantage for shaman), improved ritual activity, superior eyesight (an advantage for hunters), better sexual experiences, and increased language.

23 - Doomsday Fear photo

The Maya Doomsday Prediction—
December 21, 2012

"Don't worry about the world coming to an end today. It is already tomorrow in Australia."

Charles M. Schultz

The biggest questions of the Maya mysteries are . . . . Did the Maya really predict the End of Days? Does the end of their Long Count calendar really define the end of the world? What did the Maya really think about "The End of Times"?

End of the world theories and debates have been around since the start of the Christian era. It certainly makes sense that something beyond ourselves created us, so as easily as we were created, we could be destroyed. The end of the world date for all religions is revealed when the moment for a higher spirit rises to the heavens, calling with it its devout followers and many world end predictions have previously come to pass. Some had to do with religious interpretations and some had to do with the collapse of technology. The 2012 prediction is another theory that may come to pass or not.

Hollywood movies such as "2012", "Apocalypse", "Revelation", "I Am Legend", and the most popular end of times movies produced in 1972 "A Thief In The Night", have capitalized on "End of Days" beliefs, but all that can be done is live life as enthusiastically as possible with hope for the future.

Michel de Nostredame, also known as Nostradamus, was a 16th-century physician who also had a penchant for writing, predicted "The End of Days" to be July 29, 1999. He penned a series of prophecies, focusing primarily on wars, disasters, and destruction. Using metaphors and mystery, Nostradamus wrote his prophecies as four line verses. His followers say he predicted the rise of Hitler, and the Apollo moon landing. His critics say his writings are nothing more than ancient horoscopes, written to tell of events that undoubtedly will occur again and again.

The founder of the religious sect of Jehovah's Witness, Charles Taze Russell, chose the year 1914 as the "End of the World". Russell's successor and mentor originally claimed the year 1878 as the second advent of Christ and claimed that the dead would rise that April. Russell believed in this prophecy and sold five clothing stores that he owned in order to prepare for the big event.

With the failure of the rapture of saints in 1878, Russell decided it was not a false prophecy, but instead an error in calculation. He re-examined the doctrines of his predecessors. He then determined that Christ had indeed returned in 1878, but had been invisible to his followers, and predicted that a period he called "The Gentle Times" would end in 1914 with Christ taking over power of the earth's affairs. When World War I broke out in 1914, Russell believed that to be the beginning of the end of the world. Certainly WWI was an event large enough to spark fear and be believed as an "End of Days" to those who strongly believed.

Most recently making headlines in 2011 was "The Rapture". Its origins are from the 19th century beginning with a young girl's vision. In 1830 a Scottish girl Margaret MacDonald attended a ritual healing service. It was during this service that she claimed to have had a vision of a two stage return of Jesus Christ. Her story was amplified and adopted by a British evangelical preacher John Nelson Darby. Darby's theory eventually caught the ear of a wealthy Chicago businessman William Blackstone who promoted the idea of "The Rapture".

"The Rapture" is an idea based on three verses at the end of Chapter Nine of Daniel in The Book of Revelations in the Christian Bible. "The Rapture" is thought to be when Jesus comes to earth to save the Christians before inaugurating a seven year tribulation period beginning May 21, 2011 which was changed to October 21, 2011.

A date for the beginning of time must first be determined in order to transpire a date on our calendar for an end of times prediction. Determining a start date of creation hasn't been the easiest task to accomplish, yet alone a task that doesn't come with many debates. Scholars have not agreed upon an actual calendrical begin date.

Correlating calendars through out history is a must in determining an end of times date. Correlating the Maya calendar with the present day Gregorian calendar has been one that is filled with much confusion and discrepancy as the actual correlation of Maya to Gregorian dates has never been fully agreed upon.

The Gregorian calendar that we currently use has undergone intense and many changes for humans all over the world to measure a day, a week, a year, the seasons, and Christian holidays. It was introduced in 1582 by Pope Gregory XIII. He brought together a commission of astronomers and senior Catholic Church officials to fix the errors of the Julian calendar. Not all countries converted from the previous Julian calendar to the Gregorian calendar right away. Some countries waited as long as one hundred years from its introduction to make the switch and some countries created and stuck to their own calendars.

The history of the Gregorian calendar is one of compromise and correction. It was derived from the Julian calendar that Julius Caesar incorporated in 45 B.C. Although Julius was a Roman, it was his love affair and passion for the legendary Cleopatra that was the deciding factor for adapting the Egyptian calendar, which was based on solar cycles to their affection for the sun, over the Roman calendar, which was based on lunar cycles. Caesar made changes to the Egyptian calendar with the intent of aligning his new calendar to the vernal equinox by adding eighty days to it and making the year 45 B.C. as the "The Year of Confusion".

When Caesar passed in 44 B.C. his successor Emperor Augustus Caesar made corrections to the Julian calendar, but even the changes made by college pontiffs, priests, and politicians, the

Julian calendar was still subject to errors. It was this reformed Julian calendar that the Spanish Conquistadors brought with them to the New Worlds.

The Maya used many calendars, but the Long Count calendar is where scientists turn to find the end of days. The truth is the Maya had stopped using the Long Count calendar before the arrival of the Spanish Conquistadors, and the Julian calendar that the Spanish brought with them were of no use to Maya. The Long Count had been replaced by an abbreviated system and unfortunately, no one knew how to integrate the new system with the Long Count system. After the fall of and abandonment of the great southern cities, Maya dates are rare and archaeologists are forced to look to remnants of history preserved by the jungles.

What is the real meaning behind the Maya Long Count calendar absence of continuation? Did the Maya see this as an end of days or is it modern society's interpretation? Maya philosophy was a belief in the cyclical nature of time, and the fifth age of the sun is a symbolic message of the return of the first father, and his son will become the fifth sun. The Maya were not caught up in a debate of seasons, as the Long Count calendar is not based on a sun cult; however, it was a direct measurement between earthly cycles and the processional cycles of the cosmos.

Western civilization got caught up in the Egyptian's sun cult and has inherited its significant inaccuracies and lost metaphors within the calendar. The conversion of the Maya Long Count calendar by calculating the Julian and Gregorian calendar years is a meshing of all three calendars.

There are four principles of correlation: developments of sculpture and architecture, inscribed dates on monuments, traditional history written in Maya books, and astronomical time. Several attempts have been made to bring about an agreement of opinions of the Maya and European chronology with widely varying results. Most attempts were made by developing a single line of evidence, and some were based on assumptions that can now be discredited. No single line of evidence should be deemed sufficient enough to decide the all important question. When is the end of times?

The Gregorian date of December 21, 2012 is one that was derived by Eric Thompson, and his associates Goodman and Martinez (GMT). His correlation is based on three post conquest documents of the Yucatán: Chronicle of Oxcutzcab, Book of Chilam Balam, and the writings of the controversial Spanish Bishop Diego de Landa. The GMT correlation is publicly the most accepted theory with the beginning of times starting at September 6, in the year 3114 B.C.

The GMT correlation of dates is one that has strong opponents, which have until recently taken the back seat to Thompson's theory. Herbert Joseph Spinden, a long time opponent of the GMT correlation, looked to a process known as Carbon-14 dating to arrive at his correlation date. Spinden's date for the correlation of the Long Count Maya calendar end was 260 years earlier than Thompson's date putting the apocalyptical day in the year 1752.

Carved wooden lintels excavated in the city of Tikal, Guatemala were examined using Carbon-14 dating, which became available after the arrival of atomic research, and fell almost exactly within the period attributed to them by the Spinden chronology. Radioactive Carbon-14 particles exist in the atmosphere and by comparing the amount of radioactive carbon in decaying matter when it is excavated, its original ratio indicates the span of time from the date of the death to the point that its remains are examined and from that the calculation of historic period can be within reasonable accuracy. Using Carbon-14 dating, Spinden's beginning of time date is November 11, 3374 B.C.

Other scientists have tried without success to pinpoint the beginning and end of time dates, but the Spinden correlation is the one with the most scientific leverage. It is no secret that Thompson and Spinden disagreed on the correlation of dates. Thompson's view of Carbon-14 dating was: "The uncritical acceptance of the new Carbon-14 process savored too much dancing 'round the Golden Calf for my liking."

Despite Spinden's advances in Carbon-14 dating, the GMT correlation is the theory with the most support. Thompson's larger than life aura had an appeal to those around him. He was quick to discredit and dismiss ideas that did not correspond with his own, and he has even been accused of manipulating evidence that would disprove his theories and ideas.

The fact that Spinden talked non-stop and his persona of not being a gentleman, quickly discredited him even though he had the scientific evidence of Carbon-14 processing. Anthropologist and author Judith Ann Remington, states "actually the GMT correlation does not fit the astronomical evidence very well. It usually requires a fairly major amendment of the Venus Table text of the Dresden Codex" and she continues by stating "when Carbon-14 dating process became available it supported the Spinden correlation, and that the GMT correlation was accepted perfunctorily at a time when the Spinden correlation was being rejected because of his ungentlemanly ways."

Even with two apocalyptical dates chosen, the correlation of the Maya count from the books of the Chilan Balam with the European calendar is not as certain as might be desired, but the possibility of error seems to be greater than about four years. Gregorian calendrical reckonings depend on the birth of Christ, solar, lunar, and seasonal reckonings and as previously discussed, the Gregorian calendar is not absolutely accurate.

The birth of Jesus Christ is what is thought to separate B.C. from A.D., but if that is true, then the birth of Christ would be the first day of the first month of the year zero, however, since the Romans and Egyptians did not use the concept of zero, the year Zero does not exist. With the absence of the year zero, the last decade of B.C. and the first decade of A.D. only contain nine years each. 1 B.C to 1 A.D. is only one year. This means that two years are missing.

No one is actually quite sure on the exact date of the birth of Jesus. This date is also a mystery, and needs to be calculated from numerous events occurring in the bible from the Roman census and the death of King Herod to the reign of Caesar Augustus and celestial occurrences of the constellations of Virgo, Leo, and the sun. When figuring the birth of Jesus, the birth of John the Baptist, the date of the Crucifixion, and the visibility of the "Star of Bethlehem" must be taken into consideration. With all of these variables it is hypothesized that the birth of Jesus was circa 4 B.C.

World end prophecies of the Maya don't end with calendar reckonings, but also take into account astronomical events that correspond with Gregorian dates. Doomsdayers claim that on December 21, 2012 there will be a great galactic alignment and that the winter solstice point and the centerline of the galaxy will line up exactly on this date. (This event actually occurred in 1998.) Earth will be in the center of the Milky Way's "dark rift" and this will cause cataclysmic events between the heavens and earth. (Each December, the earth, sun, and galactic center are roughly aligned and during the winter solstice of 2012, a planetary alignment will not be present.)

Astronomy however, does not support a match between the thirteenth baktun of the Maya Long Count calendar and the date of a galactic alignment. Astronomically, there is no precise distinction of the Milky Way's edges. The edges are vague and depend solely upon clarity of view. The dark rift of the Milky Way is simply due to giant dust clouds in the plane of our galaxy and there is nothing extraordinary about the position of the sun entering this region. The center of the Milky Way, including the "black hole" is much too far away (30,000 light years) to have any considerable effect upon the earth.

Other celestial events suspected to happen by Doomsayers in December 2012 include solar flares, solar eclipse, and Venus transits. Solar flares from sunspots can have an effect on Earth's outer radiation belt and disrupt communications, aviation, and power lines, but in 2008 despite a quiet phase for the sun, earth was bombarded with intense solar winds. A Venus transit occurred in 2004, with the next transit of Venus expected on June 5th and 6th of 2012, six months short of December 21st. The next transits of Venus after that aren't anticipated until December 11, 2117 and again on December 8, 2125.

Considering that Spinden's date of 1752 was without celestial events that the Maya would have thought to be important, certainly makes room for Thompson's December 21, 2012 date, but with the knowledge that our calendar is approximately four years ahead of time, this puts Spinden's date back to 1748. In 1748 Halley's Comet made an appearance, there was both a solar and lunar eclipse, and high sunspot activity was observed. The winter of 1748 was extremely long and tough and the summer of 1748 had unusually high temperatures. Taking Thompson's 2012 date back four years to 2008, there was little astronomical significant happenings. There were a few meteor showers and a total lunar eclipse early in the year. 2008 had its share of memorable tornadic activity in the U.S.

Perhaps the mystery of debate can be found in the Acapulco Monkey petroglyph found in recent years in Acapulco, Mexico by Mexican archeologists. The petroglyph is said to date back to 2000 B.C. It bears the long count date of 3.3.4.3.2 and corresponds with Spinden's correlation of dates which is why this glyph is so important. Neither Thompson nor Spinden were alive when the petroglyph was found and it is interesting to imagine what the two experts would say about it.

SECRETS OF THE MONKEY

"long count" date
3.3.4.3.2

"Year 3 Monkey" = 2168 BC

KEY

■ The monkey is a representation of the Mayan god Quetzalcoatl, who is an allegory for rebirth

■ The star represents Venus

■ dots represent dates in the Mayan calendar

■ Mushroom

24 - Acapulco Monkey

We are soon approaching the December 21, 2012 apocalypse date and despite the weather, celestial events, and earthly disasters in 1748 and 2008, all of the above could certainly be viewed as a means to an end of humanity. From recent earth shaking quakes ranging from New Zealand, Chile, and Japan, deadly tsunamis, to volcanic activity, humanity is fighting the forces of nature to co-exist. Unlike the Maya, today we use media attention, scientific calculations, and our ability to prepare for disaster to spotlight earthly chaos, while weather patterns, hurricanes, droughts, rainy seasons, all remain cyclical.

The Maya did not conceptualize the world as we do today and the Maya knew and studied weather patterns. Perhaps when they quit tracking long count dates, abandoned their cities, and saw the arrival of the Spanish, they realized the end of their world had come, but humanity had continued without them.

Regardless of the 2012 debate, Maya scholars and natives dismiss the apocalyptic theories, noting that end of the calendar would be regarded as a time of celebration, much like modern day New Year festivities. In fact, they believe it's a time of great celebration and luck when the planet lasts through a full Great Cycle. With that, the next Great Cycle will quietly begin anew. Humanity has made safe passage through past Great Cycles and the world is still turning. There are no known Maya inscriptions or writings that predict the end of the world when the Great Cycle concludes.

Proponents of an impending December doomsday, however, still believe our world will end and all living things will die, while others believe it will signify a time of great spiritual awakening or a massive shift in global consciousness. But is this monumental turn of a vast page in the Maya Long Count calendar really going to end the world or radically alter worldwide perspectives? Most scholars see this theory as an example of extremists using misinformation and scare tactics to profit off the fears of others or create an overdue apocalyptic event to fit their own pre-existing belief system.

What will happen on Dec. 21, 2012? It's likely that the day will pass with no major events at all. People may not even realize it's the projected doomsday, although that's unlikely considering the media attention and press it has received. We'll just have to wait and see what happens—and hopefully still be here to update this chapter on Dec. 22, 2012.

We are currently in the fourth cycle of The Maya Great Age. It is believed to be the unification of the four that have preceded it and is symbolized by a glyph that means 'shift'. At the moment according the Mayan calendar, we are traveling through the 13th baktun cycle and this final period, 1618 to 2012 A.D. (GMT), and was known by the Maya as the "triumph of materialism and transformation of matter". They predicted that this would be the time of great forgetting in which humanity drifts far away from its sense of "oneness" with nature.

The Collapse of the Maya

The Classic Maya Collapse refers to the decline and abandonment of the classic periods. Fallen cities in the southern lowlands of Mesoamerica between the eighth and ninth centuries is one of the biggest mysteries in archaeology. Profound heights reached culturally before the collapse and the relative suddenness of the collapse itself make it so intriguing.

The entire glory of the Maya empires came to an end between 800 A.D. and 925 A.D. for reasons undetermined, although possible speculations are the exhaustion of agricultural land, changes in climate, and a rebellion of the lower classes against their rulers. Maya culture slipped into decline while their cities and ceremonial centers were abandoned and in time hidden by the jungles.

The following fifty years isolated groups remained in the area. Their cultural level was low since all those who understood the calendar and the keepers of various types of knowledge were gone taking proper culture with them.

The legacy of the ancient Maya Civilization does not lie exclusively in the stone architecture of their city. Experts have many speculations for the disconnection of the ancient societies. Major revolt by the masses seems to be the most favored. Tulum was deserted and there was a loss in technical and artistic superiority. The ancient Maya history is full of examples of regions rising in status and later falling into near abandonment. Huge city-states emerged into grandness only later to deteriorate and be superceded by others. The study of the ancient Maya history indicates that a major disruption occurred in their world from 975 A.D to 1200 A.D. The introduction of new cultural elements that were foreign to their culture had a devastating effect. During this period the first Toltec features appear in Maya architecture of Uxmal and Kabah. Later places such as Izama, Mayapan, Thiho, Chompoton, and Tayasal all reached a high point with a combination of Maya and Toltec influences. Perhaps Tulum was lost to the Toltec forces of prestige.

More than eighty theories have been identified in an attempt to explain the Classic Maya Collapse and a universal theory has not been accepted. The collapse of the early societies only evokes mystery. If they were at such a high degree of excellence, how come their societies didn't last? There are many theories to the downfall of the Maya civilization; drought, famine, invasion, epidemic illness, social uproar, but the truth is unknown. The collapse is most likely due to a succession of variant systemic occurrences. Many civilizations in the Old World also have prospered and perished over the centuries, such as Rome and Troy. Perhaps the answer lies in the cataclysmic and dynamic pursuits of the human race.

The drought theory, which has become the most accepted in the last few decades, holds that rapid climate change in the form of severe drought brought about the Classic Maya collapse. Evidence for a major drought is convincing, but the big collapse occurred in the wettest parts of the Maya regions, not the much drier north.

The Maya area was considered relatively wet until around 500 B.C. 475 B.C to 250 B.C. was dry, with wetter conditions returning after 250 B.C. Drought, however, had returned again from 125 A.D to 250 A.D. Studies of Yucatán lake sediment cores have provided definitive evidence for a severe 200 year drought starting approximately 760 A.D, peaking around 800 A.D. and lasting until 1000 A.D. The latest period was the most severe occurring precisely at the time of the Maya collapse.

An array of analyzed climatic, historical, hydrologic, tree ring, volcanic, geologic, lake bed, and archeological research, and demonstrated that a prolonged series of droughts most likely caused the Classic Maya Collapse. The drought theory provides a comprehensive explanation by the effects that prolonged drought would have caused the Classic Maya civilization.

The tropical soils of thin limestone became unworkable when deprived of water and forest cover. Mega droughts hitting the Yucatan Peninsula and other basin areas were particularly intense as even a regular seasonal drought was enough to dry up surface water.

Climatic changes causing drought have been found to be major drivers in the rise and fall of civilizations all over the world. Climatic modeling, tree ring data, and historical climate data show that cold weather in the Northern Hemisphere is associated with drought in Mesoamerica. Northern Europe suffered extremely low temperatures around the same time as the Maya droughts. The same connection between drought in the Maya areas and extreme cold in northern Europe was found again at the beginning of the twentieth century.

Mesoamerican civilization provides a remarkable exception: civilization prospering in the tropical swampland. The Maya are often conceived as having lived in a rainforest, but technically, they lived in a seasonal desert without access to stable sources of drinking water. The exceptional accomplishments of the Maya are all the more remarkable because of the engineered response to the fundamental environmental difficulty of relying upon rainwater rather than permanent sources of water. Water and civilization were vitally connected in ancient Mesoamerica. It is believed water management and access were critical to the development of Maya civilization.

Critics of the drought theory wonder why the southern and central lowland cities were abandoned while the northern cities of the Yucatan continued to thrive. They also point to current weather patterns: much heavier rainfall in the southern lowlands compared to the lighter amount of rain in the northern Yucatan. Drought theory supporters state that the entire regional climate changed, including the amount of rainfall, so that modern rainfall patterns are not indicative of rainfall from 800 A.D. to 900 A.D. A significant rise in sea level along the coast nearest the southern Maya lowlands was found, coinciding with the end of the Classic period, and indicating climate change.

The archaeological evidence of the Toltec intrusion into the Yucatán suggests the theory of foreign invasion. The latest hypothesis states that non-Maya groups whose homelands were in the gulf coast lowlands invaded the southern lowlands. This invasion began in the ninth century A.D. and within one hundred years destroyed the Classic Maya.

Spanish conquistadors brought with them new settlement plans, civil and religious order, distilled alcohol, the Roman alphabet, smallpox, influenza, and the measles. Although the Maya were a broken society by the time the Spanish arrived, their arrival indeed had an impact on Maya culture and beliefs. There were hundreds and thousands of Maya who fought against the Spaniards, the Spanish prevailed. Survivors then were concentrated in areas where there were stable water supplies.

Most Mayanists do not believe that foreign invasion was the main cause of the Classic Maya Collapse. Teotihuacan influence across the Maya region may have involved some form of military invasion, however it has been noted that significant Teotihuacan-Maya interactions date from at least the Early Classic period, well before the episodes of Late Classic collapse. Mayanists have theorized that no military defeat can explain or be the cause of the lengthy and complex Classic Collapse process.

The Spanish came in 1527 A.D. but it wasn't until 1697 A.D. that they subdued the last Maya territories. That gave them almost two centuries to observe independent Maya societies. The ancient Maya cities were not in classic form upon the arrival of the Spanish voyagers. Upon their arrival, they found a poor divided land that was but a deficient reflection of its previous brilliance. The Spanish tried to systematically destroy the ancient Maya civilization. They burned codices, which contained information that will forever be a mystery. Efforts to truly understand their amazing culture have been confined due to the destruction of their cultural history. Spain and its European counterparts derived tremendous wealth from their Maya slave labor, who worked on extraordinary large agricultural estates and huge mining operations. Their society was distributed into an established social class characteristic of medieval European feudalism.

During and after the Spanish conquest, the stories and tradition of the Maya continued to be handed down to succeeding generations, albeit much influenced and limited by the influx of European practices and beliefs, Roman Catholicism in particular.

Many Maya experienced persecution for their beliefs and political oppression for centuries after the first European arrivals. There can be no doubt that Maya society and tradition has undergone substantial change, but many of the remaining Maya people today maintain an identity which is very much informed by their collective history, traditions, and beliefs.

Wars between separate kingdoms, attempts of cities within a kingdom to secede by revolting against the capital, civil wars to over throw kingships, and fights between commoners over land were the types of wars the Maya fought. Maya warfare was intense, chronic, and unable to be resolved because limitations of food supply and transportation made it impossible for any Maya city to unify the whole region in an empire. Wars had become more intense and frequent at the time of the Classic Collapse.

Maya nobles did not heed long term problems. The kings and nobles failed to recognize and solve obvious problems weakening their society. Their attention was concentrated on short term concerns of enriching themselves, waging wars, erecting monuments, and demanding peasants to support these activities. When divine kings were unable to deliver order or stability in their kingdoms doubt would have ensued within their city. Since the Maya heavily depended upon ritual led by kings, when the rains fell at the wrong time or winds and locusts destroyed the crops, this led the people to doubt their sanctimonious leaders.

Revolutions, peasant revolts, and social turmoil indeed changed things, and are typically followed by foreign wars, but there have not been documented revolutions that would have caused complete abandonment of entire regions. When lower classes or different cultural groups successfully revolt, they assume higher positions of society and bring the elite class lower. They do not leave. Apparent collapses of cities were merely "power cycling" with particular cities becoming more powerful rather than declining or being conquered.

Professor of Archeological Anthropology, Penn State, David Webster believes that populations should have increased, rather than decreased due to the lack of elite power as the elite only made up for ten percent of the population in cities, and the remaining ninety percent was made up of commoners. If large rebellions occurred, there were plenty of farmers that would have survived and new forms of hierarchical societies would have been rebuilt. It is not understood why governmental institutions were not remade following the revolts, which happened after similar events in other places such as China.

Warfare, revolution, civil war, internecine warfare, peasant revolt, and dynastic struggle are all historical phenomenon that normally resolve themselves and re-establish equilibrium. Social turmoil self corrects over time. These theories for the Classic Collapse have no historical precedent. Revolutions typically revitalize and make nations stronger. As the social and economic pendulum swings back they tend to be the opposite.

Archaeological evidence indicates that Maya building and expansion projects were at their peak from circa 730 A.D. to 790 A.D. with constant enlargement and building without any machines or beneficial tools to assist them. During this same time period, signs of the collapse of Maya civilizations were beginning to appear. The majority of the burden was placed on peasant workers in the cities to build bigger ball courts and buildings. Mayanist J. Eric S. Thompson speculated that the collapse of the Classic Maya was due to revolution among the lower Maya social classes. According to his line of thinking, as life became more burdensome work began to "undermine the religious development and collective enterprise of ordinary people". Increased burden of work may have caused the people to abandon their values and revolt against the elite of society. Thompson's theory of a peasant revolt based in part, on overtaxing people in terms of labor demands in building elite architecture does not answer the question of where all the people went, but it might help explain the abrupt collapse of elite function, as well as unfinished buildings and ceremonial centers.

Maya archeology expert Professor Elliot Abrams used quantitative reasoning to determine actual labor costs of construction by measuring the time it took to build these large structures. A single building could be built over a period of sixty to one-hundred days using approximately eighty to one-hundred-thirty workers participating in the project. He concludes that buildings did not actually need the extensive amount of time and workers to complete their large constructions. In general, the labor demand for architectural projects themselves wouldn't have led to revolt; however, the commissioning of a large building project by an arrogant or stubborn king may have been the last straw. In a broader context, it was ecological mismanagement and agriculture failure that ultimately was the problem.

Ecological theories of the Maya decline focus on the worsening agriculture and resource conditions in the Late Classic period. It was originally thought that the majority of Maya agriculture was dependent on a simple slash-and-burn system. In 1921 the hypothesis of soil exhaustion was based on this method. Similar soil exhaustion assumptions are associated with erosion, intensive agricultural, and savanna grass competition.

Recent investigations show a complicated variety of intensive agricultural techniques utilized by the Maya, explaining the high population of the Classic Maya cities which is why modern archaeologists now understand the complex, prolific, and radical agricultural techniques of the ancient Maya, several of which have not been reproduced. Intensive agricultural methods were developed and utilized by all the Mesoamerican cultures to boost their food production and give them a competitive advantage over less skillful people. Their methods included canals, terracing, raised fields, and ridged fields. The use of human feces as fertilizer, seasonal swamps, dikes, dams, irrigation, water reservoirs, several types of water storage systems, hydraulic systems, and other agricultural techniques which have not yet been fully understood. Systemic ecological collapse is said to be evidenced by deforestation, erosion, and the decline of organic assortment.

The techniques utilized by the Maya were entirely dependent upon sufficient supplies of water. The Maya thrived in what most people would consider uninhabitable territory. Their success over two millennia in this environment was astonishing. The self induced ecological collapse model gives little credit to the Maya and misrepresents the scale of environmental damage they could do to themselves in the absence of global climate change.

The thought that growing cities possibly grew faster than the agricultural capabilities of the farmers is due in part to an influx of people arriving from outside regions. The increased population and less room to farm may have led to serious food shortages and even starvation. A Maya peasant could only produce twice the needs for himself and family. At least 70% of Maya society consisted of peasants.

These factors combined with the cost of administration of cities that were at war with their neighbors and could have been too much for their civilization to withstand. The civilization abruptly collapsed around 900 A.D. One widely accepted explanation for the demise of the Maya civilization is that the population grew too big for the surrounding lands to support. Recent studies confirm massive deforestation and soil erosion just before the city's collapse. Although Maya speaking people continued to live in some areas, and still do so today, their cities were completely abandoned.

They succeeded in creating a civilization in a seasonal desert by creating a system of water storage and management, which was totally dependent on consistent rainfall. The constant need for water kept the Maya on the edge of survival. Given this precarious balance of wet and dry conditions, even a slight shift in the distribution of annual precipitation can have serious consequences.

The decline of the Maya could be related to the collapse of their complex trade systems, especially those directly connected to the Central Mexican cities of Teotihuacán. Existing knowledge of the chronology of Mesoamerica, Teotihuacán was considered to have fallen during 700 A.D. to 750 A.D., causing the "restructuring of economic relations throughout highland Mesoamerica and the Gulf Coast". This reconstruction between civilizations would have put the collapse of the Classic Maya at a slightly later date. It is now believed that the most substantial Teotihuacán influence took place during the forth and fifth centuries. In addition, the civilizations of Teotihuacán started to lose its power, and quite possibly even abandoned the city, during 600 A.D. to 650 A.D. This contradicts the previous belief that Teotihuacán power diminished during 700 A.D. to 750 A.D. Since the decline date of 600 A.D. to 650 A.D. has been widely accepted, the Maya civilizations are now thought to have survived and prospered for another century or more than what was formerly presumed. Instead of causing the collapse of the Maya, the decline of the Teotihuacán is now seen as a contributor of the sixth century hiatus.

Trade will always be influenced by significant increases or decreases of human population. The traded items between the Maya civilizations by water and land consisted mostly of luxury items rather than essential items. Most of the items traded between cities were used in everyday living and ceremonies. Edible commodities did not have a "shelf life" and thus food supplies were not made in excess in each city, shortfalls could not be overcome by trade. Even so, the energy of manual labor involved in moving mass quantities of crops would have been incredibly wasteful. The collapse of trade routes would more than likely have been temporary rather than one that resulted from failure of the entire agricultural economy. Cessation of the trade routes is a result, rather than the reason for collapse of the Classic Maya.

Classic Collapse of the Maya due to disease is speculated by some experts. Widespread disease could explain a rapid decline of populace, both directly through the spread of infection itself and indirectly as a hindrance to recover over the long run. European introductions of diseases such as small pox, typhoid, measles, cholera, and the likes do not seem like culprits as such epidemic diseases, widespread mortality, and the social disruption would have been sudden. If a European "Black Death" afflicted the Maya or impaired the Maya, extremely rapid and widespread mortality and social disruption would have been expected. Large human populations have been known throughout history to recover from such epidemics, albeit taking a few centuries.

Infectious diseases such as chagas disease and other similar diseases brought on by large intestinal roundworms caused acute and chronic diarrhoetic illnesses in the Maya. Illnesses such as these would have caused devastation to the Maya, because they would have struck a person at an early age, thereby interfering with nutritional health and the natural growth and development of a child making that individual more susceptible to other diseases later in life.

Parasitic diseases and others similar to them are common over tropical rainforest regions and seen even today in people living in primitive areas with poor sanitation. It is thought by some to have been brought on by the Maya because of a "disturbed environment" through the development of agriculture and settlements. Ideas such as this could explain the role of disease as a minor reason for the Classic Maya Collapse.

Over time, the various Maya cities developed a unique and continuous set of traditions, that were associated with their societies and achievements. Despite the early tenth century monument construction, and inscription recording effectively came to an end over large areas and many centers were later abandoned. While the Maya quickly withdrew the institution of kingship and keeping with the long count calendar, they endured and continued to maintain their assorted beliefs and traditions. The maintenance of these traditions can be seen in the relics and products of those occasionally combined with other influences more characteristic of the Gulf coast and central Mexican regions.

Today's Maya

"We are not myths of the past, ruins in the jungle or zoos. We are people and we want to be respected, not to be victims of intolerance and racism."

-Rigoberta Mench'u Tum, winner of the 1992 Nobel Peace Prize.

The ancient Maya are not completely extinct as descendants of their civilization are still found in isolated pockets practicing modernized versions of their ancient beliefs, minus the human sacrifice. The Maya are actually increasing in population, not dwindling in numbers. A heightened awareness that they are all one people with a glorious past and adaptability for future change may help them survive for centuries to come.

Although the Maya we associate with the ancient ruins or the Hollywood version of the Maya do not exist, the people have hardly vanished. To say that the Maya civilization disappeared is not only an inaccuracy, but also a disservice to the more than seven and a half million Maya living today north of Peru. While the city-states of the Classic Period have all been abandoned in the tenth century, the Maya did not disappear any more than the Italians did when the Roman Empire fell.

Many of the old ways of the Maya disappeared as new technology and modern influence were introduced. Just as in any melting pot city, the old ways were replaced with the new and the people have lost their roots. Throughout the past centuries of outside efforts to oppress and assimilate, some of the Maya have continued to hold onto their unique way of life. The Indians with the long hair and white flowing robes seen in the jungles are the Lacadons, the last remnants of the ancient empires who fled to the jungle when the Spanish conquistadors arrived. They have yet to assimilate with modern society.

The Maya who hold rigidly to the Maya way of life are divided into several groups north of Peru and speak about thirty different languages of non-traditional Spanish. In villages all over Mesoamerica the Mayan language and numbering system is still used, but the elaborate writing system of phonetic glyphs is no longer in use, although their efforts to maintain fundamentalism are slowly losing tradition and language. The indigenous thatched house, called 'casa de paja' are similar to what they were in the past. Many families are maize farmers and their crops of corn, beans, chili, tomatoes, and squash are still being harvested using the slash and burn cultivation method. The form of social organization seems to have remained intact in smaller outside villages, but is far removed in the larger cities.

Modern Maya religion is a colorful blend of ancient beliefs and rituals and Catholicism. Maya mythology merged with Catholicism easily because of the similarity between belief systems: both had priests, both burned incense during rituals, both worshipped images, both conducted elaborate pilgrimages based on a ritual calendar, and

25 - Today Maya

both had a hero god who died and rose from the dead. The ancient Maya gods have been replaced with painted and carved images of Catholic saints, although the oral histories passed down from generation to generation have the saints differing from their original European counterparts.

The Maya maintain a basic belief in the influence of the cosmos on human lives even today. Offerings are still made to the same religious deities in religious ceremonies that are both very traditional as well as a fusion of Catholic theology. Some devout Maya worship at mountain and cave shrines, making offerings, burning incense, and drinking ritual alcoholic drinks to pay homage to the Classic Maya gods. In agricultural rites, deities of the forest are still invoked, and it is still believed that evil winds loose in the world cause sickness and disease. They still practice the beliefs that growing certain plants near their houses will keep sinister spirits and harmful air away.

The calendars from the past and astronomy are still studied. Although the ancient calendars are not used to keep track of the days, the shamanic priests or "day keepers" use the 260-day Sacred Round count in modern times to set the dates of rituals, provide healing by identifying curses and offended ancestors, counting seeds and crystals in their divinations, and performing healing rituals.

Maya medicine is old age, and western medical science is studying many of its techniques, especially herbal remedies. The herbal medicine of today is still administered by a shaman after masterful rituals of invoking supernatural powers have been performed. They still believe that the physical body is affected by the spirit world first and by the effects of the material world secondly.

Many scientists believe that native lineages were deliberately destroyed or they falsified their own history for political reasons. Although there is more information now more than ever relating to the ancient way of life of the Maya, but there is so much more to be discovered. Research continues to unearth new facts about the early Maya civilizations, but many very real mysteries remain.

The jungles of the Yucatan Peninsula are full of temples and ruins that have yet to be identified, as well as thousands of structures in current sites that yet to be explored. Their excavation could reveal many of the secrets that still puzzle both the curious casual tourist and the dedicated archeologist. The hope for the serious ancient Maya investigator is that at the end of the day there will be answers to all these incredible questions.

Bibliography

Abrams, Elliot, University of Ohio

Abrams, Elliot. *How The Maya Built Their World*. Texas: University of Texas Press, 1994

"Ancient Scripts." http://www.ancientscripts.com/maya.html. 1996-2010

Ardren, Traci and Scott R. Hutson. *The Social Experience of Childhood in Ancient Mesoamerica*. Colorado: University Press of Colorado, 2006

"Maya Religion." *Authentic Maya*. http://www.authenticmaya.com/maya_religion.htm. 2005

Aveni, Anthony F. *Ancient Astronomers*. St. Remy Press, 1993

Baquedano. *Aztec, Inca & Maya*. Eyewitness Books, 2003

Battle, John A. Th.D., Christ In The Gospels, Chronology of Jesus' Life, Chapter 4, Western Reformed Seminary, www.wrs.edu

Bunson, Margaret R., and Stephen M. Bunson. *Encyclopedia of Ancient Mesoamerica*. New York: Facts On File, Inc., 1996.

Campbell, Lyle. "American Indian Languages: The Historical Linguistics of Native America." *Oxford Studies in Anthropological Linguistics*, no. 4. New York: Oxford University Press, 1997

Campbell, Lyle, Terrence Kaufman and Thomas C. Smith-Stark. "Meso-America as a Linguistic Area", *Language* Vol. 62, No. 3 (Sep., 1986), pp. 530-570

Cancun Ecotourism Tour, Tulum Mexico. 2 hour guided tour in Tulum, Mexico, Quinta Roo. February 2009

Castledine, David. *Tulum, The Mayas: History and Art*. Panorama Guidebooks, 1990

Christenson, Dr. Allen J. "Ancient Maya Culture." Lonely Planet Publications. http://www.lonelyplanet.com

Coe, Andrew. *Archaeological Mexico, A Traveler's Guide to Ancient Cities and Sacred Sites.* Avalon Travel Publishing, 2001

Coe, Michael. *Native Astronomy in Mesoamerica in Archaeoastronomy in Pre-Columbian America.* U. of Texas Press, 1975

Coe, Michael D. *The Maya.* Thames & Hudson, 2005, Seventh Edition

Conrad, David. "The Ancient Maya—A Commercial Empire." *Mex Connect* http://www.mexconnect.com/articles/1574-the-ancient-maya-a-commercial-empire. 1996-2011

Criscenzo, Jeeni. "The Maya Calendar." http://www.criscenzo.com/jaguarsun/calendr.html. 1997-2000

de Borhegyi, Carl

de Borhegyi, Carl. "Hidden In Plain Sight." www.mushroomstone.com

de Bourgoing, Jacqueline. *The Calendar—History, Lore, and Legend.* Harry N. Abrams, Inc., 2001

Deschense, David. "Christ's Real Birthdate." *Fort Fairfield Journal.* (Nov. 21, 2007): p. 9. http://www.mainemediaresources.com/mpl_christbirthdate.htm

"Dictionary of Art Historians." http://www.dictionaryofarthistorians.org

Diamond, Jared. *Collapse, How Societies Choose to Fail or Succeed.* Viking-Penguin Group, 2005

Douglas, Bruce L. DDS. "A Re-evaluation of Guedel's Stages of Anesthesia." http://www.ncbi.nlm.nih.gov/pmc/articles/PMC2067263/pdf/jadsa00141-0011.pdf

Duncan, David Ewing. *Calendar—Humanity's Epic Struggle To Determine a True Year and Accurate Year.* Avon Books, Inc., 1998

Dunham, Will. "Feeling Blue? Not Like a Maya Sacrificial Victim." Rueters, http://www.reuters.com/article/2008/02/27/us-maya-blue-idUSN2742908120080227. Feb. 2008

Early Spanish Expeditions to Mexico. http://mexicanhistory.org/

Espenak, Fred, NASA.GSFC. "2004 and 2012 Transits of Venus.",http://eclipse.gsfc.nasa.gov/transit/venus0412.html. 2002

Gallenkamp, Charles. *Maya: The Riddle and Rediscovery of A Lost Civilization.* David McKay Company, Inc., 1959

Gilbert, Adrian and Maurice Cotterell. *The Maya Prophecies.* Element Books, 1995

Grun, Bernard. *Timetables of History, A Horizontal Linkage of People and Events.* Touchstone: Simon and Schuster, 1963

Hartley, C. http://users.hartwick.edu/hartleyc/mayacalendar.html. 2003

Historical Events. www.hisdates.com

Houston, Stephen D. *Extract from: Function and Meaning in Classic Maya Achitecture.* Dumbarton Oaks. www.doaks.org/etexts.html. 1998

Hurst, K Kris. "Maya Civilization Important Facts." *About.com.* http://archaeology.about.com/od/mayaarchaeology/a/maya_civ_3.htm

Idaho State University. "Time, Timekeeping, Calendars." www.physics.isu.edu

Indians.org. "Mayan Civilization." http://www.indians.org/welker/maya.htm

Jenkins, Dawn E. "Orion in MesoAmerica." *Astra's Star Gate.* http://www.astras-stargate.com/orion.htm

Jenkins, Major, John. "Transcendence in Mayan Mythology." *Meaning of the 5th Sun in Mayan Mythology.* http://www.siloam.net/jenkins

Jenkins, Major John. "Alignment 2012." http://alignment2012.com

Johson, Kenneth. "The Mayan Philosophy of Numbers." www.maya-portal.net. Nov 2009

León-Portilla, Miguel. *Time and Reality in the Thought of the Maya.* 1988. Second Edition

Marusek, James A. "Impact." www.breadandbutterscience.com

Matthews, Ruppert. *You Wouldn't Want To Be a Mayan Soothsayer, Fortunes You'd Rather Not Tell.* Scholastic: Franklin Watts, 2008

"Maya Gods and Goddesses." *Crystal Links.* http://www.crystalinks.com/mayangods.html

Maya sites in Quintana Roo: Tulúm." *Athena Review* Vol.2, no.1, 2003, webpage: AthenaPub-Tulum. http://www.athenapub.com/tulumint.htm

"The Mayan Calendar", http://survive2012.com
"The Mayan Calendar." *Calendars Through the Ages.* http://www.webexhibits.org/calendars/calendar-mayan.html. 2008

"Mayan Religion." *Religion Facts.* http://www.religionfacts.com/mayan_religion/index.htm. 2004-2010

Bonnie Bley

Mayan Timelines. http://mayankids.com

Mayan World.com. http://www.mayan-world.com

Meyer, Peter. "The Julian and Gregorian Calendars." *Hermetic Systems* http://www.hermetic.ch/cal_stud/cal_art.html

Miller, Bill. "The Great 2012 Doomsday Scare." www.nasa.gov

Miller, Mary and Karl Taube. *An Illustrated Dictionary of the Gods and Symbols of Ancient Mexico and the Maya.* London: Thames and Hudson Ltd, 1993

Missouri State University History Department, http://history.missouristate.edu/

Montgomery, David. *Dirt: The Erosion of Civilizations.* California:University of California Press, 2007

Morley, Sylvanus Griswald. *An Introduction to the Study of Maya Hieroglyphs.* Dover Publications, 1975

Moskowitz, Clara. "Secret to Mayan Blue Paint Found." *Live Science.* http://www.livescience.com/2322-secret-mayan-blue-paint.html. 2005

Mundo Maya Online. http://www.mayadiscovery.com/ing/archaeology/palenque/kings/

Mythic Imagination. www.mythicjourneys.org

NASA. www.nasa.gov

Neto, Frederico. "Sustainable Tourism, Environmental Protection and Natural Resource Management: Paradise on Earth?" http://unpan1.un.org/intradoc/groups/public/documents/un/unpan002600.pdf. United Nations, 2002

Nicholson, Irene. *Mexican and Central American Mythology.* Random House Value, 1976

O'Dell, C. Robert. *The Orion Nebula—Where Stars Are Born.* The Bellnap Press, 2003

"Other Ancient Calendars." *Calendars Through the Ages.* http://www.webexhibits.org/calendars/calendar-ancient.html. 2008

Penton, M. James. *Apocalypse Delayed: The Story of Jehovah's Witness.* Canada:University of Toronto Press, 1997, 2nd Edition

Pinto, Nick. "Revelation 2012, What If The Apocalypse Already Happened?" *Minneapolis City Pages,* April 2011, pg 9-15

Powers, George W. *Important Events, A Book of Dates.* 1899

"Quetzalcoatl: Man Or Myth?." *123HelpMe.com* http://www.123HelpMe.com/view.asp?id=82876. Aug 23, 1011

Raymo, Chet. *365 Starry Nights—An Introduction to Astronomy for Every Night of The Year.* Simon & Schuster, 1982

Richards, E.G. *Mapping Time—The Calendar and Its History.* New York: Oxford University Press, 1998

Rossing, Barbara R. *The Rapture Exposed, The Message of Hope in The Book of Revelation.* Westview Press, 2004

"Santos of New Mexico." http://www.collectorsguide.com/fa/fa077.shtml

Saunders, Nicholas J. *The Peoples of the Caribbean: An Encyclopedia of Archeology and Traditional Culture.* ABC-CLIO, 2005

Schele, Linda and David A. Freidel. *A Forest of Kings: The Untold Story of the Ancient Maya.* Harper Perennial, 1992

Schele, Linda and others. *The Code of Kings: the Language of Seven Sacred Maya Temples and Tombs.* Simon and Schuster, 1999

Sharer, Robert J. and Loa P. Traxler. *The Ancient Maya.* California: Stanford University Press, 2006

Sidrys, Raymond V. "Classic Maya Obsidian Trade." *American Antiquity, Society for American Archaeology.* Vol. 41. No. 4. (Oct. 1976): 449-464

Smithsonian National Museum of History Anthropology Department. "Unmasking The Maya." http://anthropology.si.edu/maya/

"Spanish Conquest of Yucatán." http://en.wikipedia.org/wiki/Spanish_conquest_of_Yucat%C3%A1n

Spinden, Herbert Joseph. *Ancient Civilizations of Mexico and Central America.* New York: Library of Congress, 1917

Tedlock, Dennis. *Popol Vuh, The Definitive Edition of The Mayan Book of The Dawn of Life and The Glories of Gods and Kings.* Simon & Schuster, 1996

"10 Facts on Tulum Ruins, My Tulum Travel." *The Tulum Ulitimate Guide* http://mytulumtravel.com/tulum/tulum-city-of-the-dawn/

"Tulum." http://www.playa.info/playa-del-carmen-info-mayan-ruins-of-tulum.html

"Tulum Mayan Ruins." *Different World.com* http://www.differentworld.com/mexico/areas/caribbean-coast/tulum/tulum-mayan-ruins.htm

"Tulum Ruins: A Must Visiting Historical Site." http://www.centralamericavoyage.com/tulum-ruins.html

"Tours by Mexico." http://www.tourbymexico.com/qroo/tulum/tulum.htm

Various Authors *Lost Civilization, The Magnificent Maya.* Time Life Books, 1993

Vogel, Susana. *Guide of Tulum, History, Art and Monuments.* Ediciones Monclem, 1995

Webster, David, Pennsylvania State University

Webster, David. *The Fall of the Ancient Maya: Solving the Mystery of the Maya Collapse.* Thames & Hudson Ltd, 2002

Webster, David. "Lowland Maya Fortifications." *American Philosphical Society: Proceedings of the American Philosophical Society.* Vol. 120. No. 5 (Oct 1976)

Webster, David. "The Uses and Abuses of the Ancient Maya*." Emergence of the Modern World Conference.* Otzenhauzen Germany, 2007

"When Was Jesus Born?" http://www.oration.com/~mm9n/articles/hist/christmas.htm

Wikopedia. www.wikipedia.com

Wilson, Ken. "Mayan Gods, Maya." *Lost Civilizations.* http://www.lost-civilizations.net/mayan-gods.html

Witschey, Walter R. *Muyil-Quintana Roo-Mexico.* (http://muyil.smv.org/tulum.htm). Sept. 2008

Yeomans, Dr. Donald. "A Galactic Alignment in December 2012—So What?" *Nasa Space Information.* www.nasa.gov

Young, Peter. *Secrets of the Ancient Maya.* Hatherleigh Press, 2003

Index